T0352948

African
COWRIE SHELLS
Divination

· · · · · · · · · ·

History,
Theory & Practice

About the Author

Professor of Scientific Astrology and Practice. Teacher of Mental Control. Parapsychologist Expert in divination techniques. Clairvoyant. Natural psychic. Medium. Scholar and Researcher of Primitive Cultures. Expert in Myths and Legends. TV and Radio host.

An esoteric individual who specializes in all areas of the Supernatural, although now residing in Europe, Zolrak's work has taken him all over the world, where he has given talks and run courses and conferences.

Everyone who requests his expert services (including many artists and celebrities from all over the globe) all agree that he possesses a great magical power with vast and deep esoteric knowledge. This is the reason that they call him The Magician.

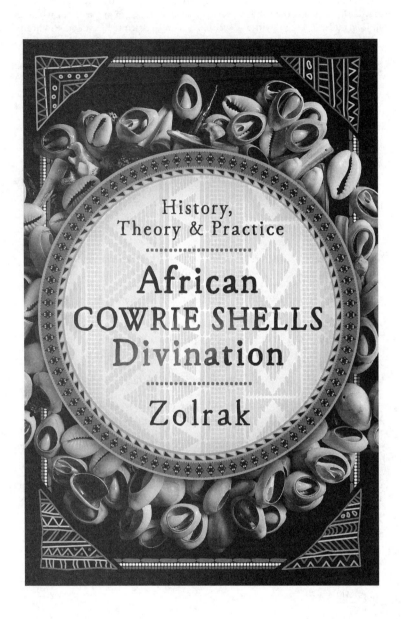

History,
Theory & Practice

African
COWRIE SHELLS
Divination

Zolrak

Llewellyn Publications
Woodbury, Minnesota

First Edition
Second Printing, 2021

Book design by Ted Riley
Cover design by Shira Atakpu
Translation by Gracie Miller

Llewellyn Publications is a registered trademark of Llewellyn Worldwide Ltd.

Library of Congress Cataloging-in-Publication Data

Names: Zolrak, author.
Title: African cowrie shells divination : history, theory, and practice /
   Zolrak.
Description: First edition. | Woodbury, Minnesota : Llewellyn Publications,
   [2019] | Includes bibliographical references.
Identifiers: LCCN 2018060955 (print) | LCCN 2019001676 (ebook) | ISBN
   9780738758596 (ebook) | ISBN 9780738758589 (alk. paper)
Subjects: LCSH: Cowries—Religious aspects. | Divination—Africa, West. |
   Divination—Caribbean Area. | Fortune-telling by shells—Africa, West. |
   Fortune-telling by shells—Caribbean Area. | Yoruba (African
   people)—Religion. | Afro-Caribbean cults. | Africa, West—Religious life
   and customs. | Caribbean Area—Religious life and customs.
Classification: LCC BF1779.C64 (ebook) | LCC BF1779.C64 Z65 2019 (print) |
   DDC 133.30966—dc23
LC record available at https://lccn.loc.gov/2018060955

Llewellyn Publications
A Division of Llewellyn Worldwide Ltd.
2143 Wooddale Drive
Woodbury, MN 55125-2989
www.llewellyn.com

Printed in the United States of America

For all those prophets and inspired ones that with just looking at a star revealed the deeper mysteries: those of life. For the big daily fortune-tellers, cheering simple things that help to keep peace and tranquility. For all people who, one way or another, understood and understand that to look at the future, present, and past is the thing of humans and gods—the only glorious moment in which the muses help us fly very high, so high that we don't even need wings. For all of them, I incline my head and I join them in the universal concert of free souls.

Contents

Diloggún Guide

Acknowledgments

To my spiritual sons and daughters, who were the ones who most encouraged me in this work.

To my illustrator and collaborator in general, Durkon, for his excellent drawings, for perfection in strokes and lines, for the richness of his colors and the intentionality of his message. For his great devotion to the Orishás, for his unconditional respect for spiritual entities and guides. For his knowledge in different branches of metaphysics, which made this hard work much more pleasant. For sharing knowledge and making it more understandable for the reading public.

To Candy of Oshún, whom destiny made me meet in the city of Chicago while we held a cycle of conferences around the United States. To her, for her tender eyes, her fresh smile, and limpid thoughts.

Especially to Cecilia Mateos Diaz, the best fortune-teller of Spanish cards of all Spain. Located in the traditional and luxurious district of Salamanca, Madrid, she displays daily the valuable Art of interpreting the future with a professional aptitude rarely seen. Dear friend, Soul Sister, thank you very much for the painstaking work and love that you give to all who come to you seeking answers and relief to their sorrows.

And to Ubirajara Pinheiro, companion and friend of other lives, and for whom I have a deep admiration and respect. For his extraordinary talent and power with which he develops in the world of divinatory arts, with his particular style, when deploying his cowrie shells along with elements such as cola nuts, coins, and other things that make up a true mystery and enigma in the supernatural world—which he performs so well on a daily basis in his practice in Rio de Janeiro, Brazil.

To all of them: Thank you. God bless you!

SPECIALLY DEDICATED TO THREE
BEINGS OF LIGHT THAT TRANSCENDED
THIS EARTHLY PLANE

······•• ◉ ••·······

CARL WESCHCKE

....

My dear Carl,

Dear friend, I know you must be very busy, despite having left us, but your soul was always restless, overflowing with healthy faith, incalculably analytical, scrutinizing, and deeply investigating.

You have left a great legacy, and only the great can achieve that. You have done it, and today you are present in the memory and the Heart of all those who had the good fortune to meet you and share with your hilarious, fantastic, and successful moments.

When I shook your hand for the first time, at that precise moment, I realized that I was in front of a Great Wizard. Not only were you the businessman and editor, but also a man who knew perfectly the intricacies of the human soul.

Your tender gaze always revealed patience, wisdom, and a certain magnetism that made you so special, even for those who could not grasp your magnitude.

From where you are, from the plane of Light that God has designated you, I am sure that you continue to inspire, encourage, and protect your loved ones, friends, and authors—because all of us believe that, without exception, we are a part of the world of your affections, because your generous soul allowed it.

Carl dear, today I embrace you from here, having the firm conviction that you are still struggling to gain knowledge and that you will surely be illuminating with your smart mind those spirits who still do not understand the true mysteries of the soul.

Until always,
Zolrak

PIERRE EDOUARD LEOPOLD VERGER

Writer, photographer, anthropologist, ethnologist, researcher of African religions, Babalawo, known simply as Pierre Verger, aka Fatumbi ("he who is reborn through Ifá"), who has been born again thanks to or through Ifá and represents the true meaning of this word.

My respected Pierre,

In the nineties, the beginning of that decade, you had the deference to share with me your home in San Salvador de Bahía, Brazil, where we spent hours talking about the Candomblé, spirituality, divination, the oracles, etc.

For me it was an honor to meet you in those times and to be able to teach the tarot of the Orishás, which in Brazil was known and known as *O Tarô Sagrado Dos Orixás.*

We talked a lot and a lot was also learned from you.

Thank you very much, dear Pierre, for your humility, your human warmth, and for all the Good that you have done for the intellectual world with your extensive and fantastic work.

You were and you will be a great one, a Legend that will remain alive.

My respects and my usual admiration,
Zolrak

JOSE RIBEIRO DE SOUZA

King of Candomblé *in Brazil, writer, lecturer, professor of Sudanese languages, recorder of allusive discs, and presenter on radio and television. Babalorixa, Spiritual Head of the Terreiro de Iansa Egun-Nita, of Estrada Santa Efigenia 152, Taquara, Jacarepagua, in Rio de Janeiro, Brazil.*

My dear father,

There are many things I have to thank you for. You were very much a spiritual father; I thank you one by one for all your religious endeavors, but also those that formed my character, and for the place you gave me next to you, under your protection and shelter.

You were a man of great Power, but your moral values made them always shine within the Good, enhancing your mission as a priest and honoring the great office that you sustained.

Your teachings are still here with me, treasured for what they are: true gems, erós, true secrets.

When some uncertainty quieted or confused me, you told me, "Son, do not forget that you are Santero." Dear Father, I have never forgotten…and I try to honor all the good feelings and the trust that you instilled in me.

I can only say to you,
ASHÉ!

Introduction

I have always considered Africa to be the most magical, mysterious, and enigmatic continent, full of supernatural forces and powerful legends, and also as the Mother Earth of all Magic, where everything originated, passed, and finally extinguished in order to start again in an uninterrupted cycle of Life beyond Life.

Africa was, is, and will continue to be the inexhaustible source of spiritual resources, where Nature expresses itself with greater intensity. Among its landscapes, everything comes to life, and even the most conservative and skeptical minds relax and end up considering what they never would have admitted as possible or true. There, the foreign becomes natural, and the natural becomes supernatural. Everything acquires extreme dimensions. Strong and powerful, behind each leaf, flower, plant, rock, or body of water, we are able to perceive the creation of God in his most refined version.

From a very young age, I was connected with Spirituality and with all spiritual phenomena and mediumnimic manifestations; my soul approached, in an accurate and very precise way, the Invisible World of the Spirits. Maybe someday I will extend myself in these topics, telling you how my thirst for Spiritual knowledge was developed and deepened in my person.

In the long journey of this learning, my investigative spirit, curiosity, and inner urgencies led me to connect with fantastic people and characters, revealing situations that were before me as if a heavy and luxurious theatrical curtain was pulled back to show before my eyes the most fantastic, tangible, and palpable reality of esoteric manifestations.

This made me start a path that I never finished doing, because every step that I make illustrates me in such a way in which I always learn and never finish thanking the Cosmos for the infinite opportunities that they have given me, taking it as a Mission of life.

I was always a believer, and I could not conceive life without the conception of the Almighty God, Love of all, Truth, and Justice. That is why I respect all the religious and philosophical currents that have these precepts, because they all carry the same ends and aim to bring us closer to the Creator.

In my background there are several titles, many of them referring to parapsychology and other branches related to it. And as a parapsychologist, I consider that I could only nourish myself from the true things, taking part and acting. The path was long, extensive, laborious, but encouraging and very rewarding.

I connected with great Teachers, which my angels were putting before me, and the time came when I needed to leave many things aside and prioritize the Mandates of the Beyond. Connecting with Africanism, I considered that the most efficient and productive way was the serious, deep, and respectful research done in a progressive, analytical, and suspect way, but that I could not do it in any way unless it was an authentic way.

And to do so, the only way was to do it from within—participating. If not, everything would have been an incomplete compilation of incomplete knowledge, as if it were different reports immersed in a certain protocol with extravagant titles but with information that is not very pragmatic and often incomprehensible.

Driven by a spiritual and intellectual impulse and need, I decided to start my journey in the Saint's Law and moved from a Kardecist spiritualism to enter and frequent the Umbanda.

I still remember the sound of drums and what they produced in me. All my skin bristled and my mind and soul flew to recondite places, entering into a trance and passionately connecting with the Spiritual in its maximum expression.

All this led me to grow within the Oyo Nation, in which my spiritual lineage comes from the house of Luis de Bara (Porto Alegre, Brazil). From that branch of culture, I received my first *jogo de búzios* (cowrie shell divination kit), which is composed of only eight cowrie shells.

I went on my way—until I met my true Mentor, a great Babalorixa, Jose Ribeiro de Souza, who was the King of Candomblé. He was my guide, my Teacher, who transmitted to me *Ashé* and increased in me the need for improvement, passion for the Orishás, and love for each and every one of the beings who approached and who would approach to find an answer, a comforting guide to face your problems and inconveniences.

And it was like that, in the year 1985, having already fulfilled all the "obligations" of one year, of three years, and five years, I was already prepared to receive my priestly rights.

Among the most precious and valuable of these Obligations is the Obligation of the Seven Years (Odu Ige), known as Deka, or Cuia in the Candomblé of Angola, which I was formed.

In that ceremony, I received all the fundamentals and the physical, material, spiritual, and intellectual tools that every high priest must have. Among those belongings and values were my jogo de búzios, consisting of sixteen cowrie shells, *pembas* (sacred and consecrated limestones), seeds, scissors, razor, etc.—all the means and tools to initiate future spiritual Sons of Saint and exercise a priesthood fully.

I still remember and I still get excited when doing it, when my Father of Saint, Jose Ribeiro, gave me my *Peneira de palha* or *Opon-MerinDiloggún*, decorated with búzios and interwoven beads in the *palha da costa*.

This delivery, known as *Cuia de Ashé*, was made in the presence of High Priests of the Candomblé, *Caciques de Umbanda* (Heads of Umbanda), and some guests, the Sons of Saint, belonging to the Temple.

Following this presentation of Cuia, my Orishá in front (the denomination that is given to the Angel of the Guardian) confirmed his presence—answering so affirmatively—when my Master raised the leaf of the plant belonging to me. My loved Oxalá, my father.

Many years have passed and I still respect the guidelines they have taught me, and I am still perfecting myself within my possibilities within this arduous path of knowledge and learning.

I take care of my two jogos de búzios with sacredness, because that is how I received them, and so they are Sacred.

My mentor told me two things. One of them was "You will be my only son, who, like me, will be a researcher and write books. And, as a writer, you will be known; you will also be on radio and television." And he was not wrong. Each one of those things I have fulfilled with great gratifications for my soul. And the second thing was "You have an Ifá Aya (Inner or Heart Oracle)" and he explained to me that he was born with certain paranormal faculties, which gave me Clairvoyance of Birth and thus the path of *Dafa* (which could be defined synthetically as the Divinatory concept within Ifá and the process of interpreting an Odú).

He considered, like many other great figures within the line of Afro-American culture, that Dafa committed to every divinatory process, and that each and every one of the currents and divinatory sources, wherever they were, were pouring and enriching each other, forming a melting pot of knowledge merging into one, the power to see beyond material barriers.

Each and every one of these things led me to write this book, but in fact the trigger was when my dear friend Carl Weschcke, who was the founder and president of Llewellyn Worldwide, in a meeting in his office, and making use of his passionate ability to enter into the feelings and souls of others, with a deep voice, slow and full of deep emotion, for being a great connoisseur of the Worlds of Mind and Spirit (only the great Men and Women have that gift), and as if drawing from his magical, intellectual galley, he asked me to do so—to write a book about this topic.

Knowing in advance that this would entail a great responsibility and commitment, his request for me was strong enough to accept the challenge, and from a place of respect and humility, I have tried to transmit everything that has been taught to me, everything that I was informed of in long investigations, conversations, and talks, many of them with "way's partners," as I like to call my friends and spiritual brothers.

Dear reader, today you know something more about me. I will try to help you very respectfully to know this World, and every time you read a page of this book, your energy will be communicating with Dafa, and through your intuition, all your perceptive abilities will increase.

The purpose is for you to connect with this Wonderful Universe of divinatory techniques, that you get involved in it, and that you get answers to your questions.

But always bear in mind that your times are not always those of God, and that He has reserved for each one of us a time and a space, where each one has a mission reserved, and that the time of God is Perfect.

The understanding of all this, and perhaps each of the words and phrases that you read, will arrive in a finished manner, at the opportune and ideal moment, and will often coincide with your current concerns and needs; perhaps others will come when you are ready for it.

When this becomes effective, it will be that God's plan is being fulfilled. It will not be before or after, but when you are ready, finely prepared for it, with incredibly perfect accuracy and precision, like everything that comes from the Creator.

Others will be able to do it immediately, and that will be simply because their Interior Master is already prepared, ready to assimilate everything immediately. But if it were not so, do not be discouraged, and do it your way, in your time, because I assure you that everything will come in the right measure, not before or after.

Many years have passed from everything that I have told you, abbreviated, and today I define myself as a Universalist who tries to understand and respect, as I previously told you, all the manifestations of Faith, of religiosity.

I try to communicate with the Divine essence of God when I meditate and try to transcend, when I enter a church to pray, when I attend a spiritual session, or simply when I am ecstatic before the Imposing and Majestic Nature.

Thank you very much for coming here and for having had the impulse and intuition sharpened by curiosity or simply the need to know by acquiring your copy of this Work.

Thank you again,

Zolrak

For Whom This Book Is Directed

Keeping in mind that beyond divinatory and predictive power, the reading of Ifá reinforces and ponders through advice and guides gathered in the stories, or *Patakkíes*, for all ethical-moral values for the proper Development and sustenance of every Society, from the individual to the collective, and the personal to the general.

From there that, opting for any method of divination, either the cowrie shells or búzios, the *Opelé de Ifá*, the *Obi*, etc., the solution and the answers will always have a moral charge, leading to recognize our shortcomings and obtain a means to correct the wrong, balance the energetic disorders, and liberate the enlightenment for growth and spiritual strengthening. For all these reasons, many consider Ifá and its system as a compilation of moral Laws, as if it were (said with much respect) a bible or African sacred book.

In general rules, and not making distinctions of any kind, this book would then be so comprehensive that it would be really intended for everyone, for all people. But doing it in a more selective or specific way, we could say that it is directed to all those who are interested in the World of Divination in general, to scholars, researchers, or the curious, who are driven by an impulse that starts from the very essence of the human being to know, to inquire, and to be in contact with the most profound reality of Knowledge. In this case, it is a knowledge of centuries, cradled in Yoruba civilization, and inherited orally from priest to priest.

That said, it is also possible to attach to the long list of interested readers the topics of anthropologists and practitioners or sympathizers of all the cultural aspects of all African American religions. As a parapsychologist, I would dare to say that any researcher of the paranormal was caught by this theme. And, of course, it will open a very diverse facet, where simply those who want or need to understand their present and reveal future events will enter.

The neophytes in the matter will find a fascinating world, instructive and revealing at the same time. I advise all of them from the depths of my Heart (because there is the genuine truth of Humankind) to approach another of my works, *The Tarot of the Orishas*, where there is an introduction and employment to another tool of divination. With this, they will come to understand more the essence of the Orishás and their manifestations.

Neophytes and initiates in this knowledge will find in this book a greater adaptation and understanding, with the *jogo de cuatro búzios*, or reading of four cowrie shells; the divination with the coconut, or Obi; and also with the *alubosa*, or onion.

The objective is not only to connect with a divinatory technique, or one of the most historically ancestral, but also to become familiar with each of the techniques, incorporate them in a practical and intellectual way, so that when resorting to them, by consulting with a *Babalorixa* (Father of Saint) or *Babalawo* (Father of the secret), one can be prepared, ready, and open to understand even more the message of the Orishás, thus reaching with total fluidity the reflections that Ifá wants or allows to transmit.

It will be, in this way, expanding the personal perception, which together with the priest, the fortune-teller, will produce a totally optimal result where there will be a perfect feedback of understanding and revelation.

For the practitioners, it will also be beneficial since the theories and knowledge of the Afro-Caribbean Santería, the Candomblé, and other different nations of culture have been combined to make these techniques more complete and comprehensible.

And finally for all the religious staff, it will be enriching, since the Work has tried to deepen the knowledge and translate it into a vocabulary of interpretation, one could say, more "Western," in a very complete but simple way.

African Divination Arts

Dear readers, I want to invite you to discover the wonderful magical world of the African divination arts—irrefutable steps to other dimensions, which for those who wish to travel them, a Universe of knowledge awaits.

Within them, there is one of the most elaborate divinatory techniques with profound mystical breadth: the fascinating and seductive language of cowrie seashells, which is one of the central themes developed in this book.

The cowrie shells are the eyes, the mouths, and the ears of the Yoruba pantheon, the eternal bonds of this ancient and wise African people with Divinity. They represent knowledge that does not escape the everyday reality of our life; on the contrary, it is intertwined with it, making clearer the messages from other spheres. They are higher levels spiritually compared to this low astral world in which we live.

No divination art is learned quickly, since each one of them carry their time of maturation and the personal process of who is integrating them as knowledge in order to be able to investigate the infinite powers of the mind and the Cosmos. Better would be the adaptation of them to ourselves—knowing how to evenly combine the intangible world of ideas and thoughts with the real and concrete world of things and objects. A good predisposition for a greater permeability to the supernatural and the unknown accelerates these processes.

There's an established challenge between our emotions, expectations, dreams, desires, baggage of our faith, and the tangible body. All of this is brought together to establish the best contact between what our consciousness needs and what the divination techniques can really provide us.

Through African divination arts, we are seeking a symbiosis between the rational and the irrational and breaking the prejudices and the preconceptions that can often interrupt the true messages of the future.

We wake up from a long dream of unhealthy coherence, many times considering as non-fantasies the things we can perceive, and that does not allow us to penetrate other dimensions of dreams and passions that materialize and exist in other planes. From that perspective, plans are born in other places that are valid, as we don't forget our divine origin as creations of a single source: the Creator.

And taking into account that all the worlds—those known to our concrete and real minds and those we can only perceive—really cohabit and intertwine. In this way it's possible to capture the power to reveal our past, present, and future through all divining arts in a fraction of time.

These arts always existed in different periods of humanity. Imperceptibly, almost with profound innocence, they opened the way so that Humankind could reach God in intention and thought. This let the soul fly to climb to the source of eternal knowledge. Only by releasing the spirit away from anger, fear, hatred, and revenge will we have taken the first step to prepare our receiving field.

Oblivious to low emotions, the inspiring muses will guide our journey in a few seconds at high levels of mystical depth—and in those few moments, we will have embraced the whole of creation. From there, the spectrum of our perception will be sharpened, and the gift of prophecy will no longer be so unattainable, because we will have the necessary secrets to deal with it seriously but at the same time with extreme humility.

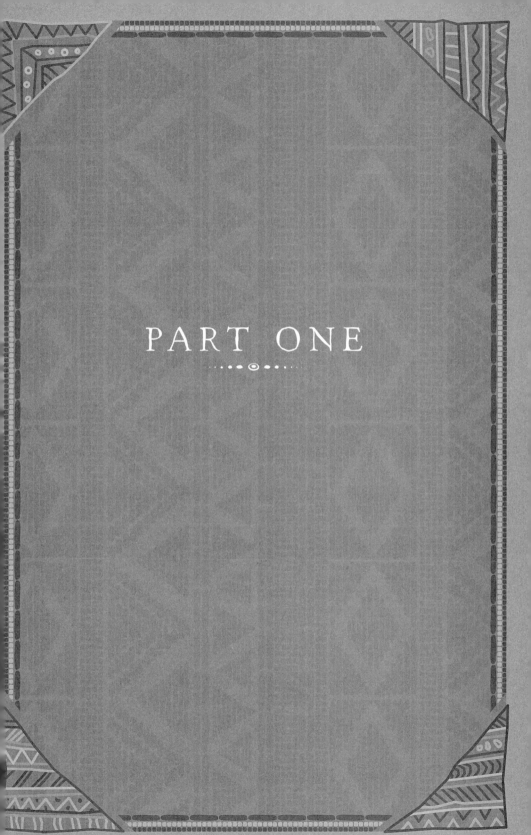

PART ONE

History and Background
of African Divination

African divination arts and their systems—the themes of our book—are some of the most revealing of all items and premises. They are like the perfect gears of a great mechanism of wisdom, talent, and prophesy. Most of them, the ones I consider more perfect from the point of view of the prophecy itself, were cradled by an ancient civilization: the Yoruba, which, until today, remains strengthened by the passage of time, safeguarded by careful caretakers of spiritual principles, and as unalterable as the nobility of the soul of its worshippers.

Their ancestors, the moral and intellectual leaders of their system of planning and appearance in the earthly world, suggest a whole solemn structure of magical simultaneity in time and space. This makes the ineffable idea of an eternal universe palpable in our hearts, indivisible with Humankind and our destiny on Earth.

According to the philosophic-religious thought of Yoruba culture, their systems of divination present different rolls or throws of various significant objects or offerings that represent the ancestral voices in the form of a reading. The souls of their ancestors are the link to a divine past, the ancestral and the present, forming two chains of forces that interact together. It's the beginning of a time when we will uninterruptedly return after our perfection and spiritual overcoming.

Each configuration of their systems of divination forms magical chains that, as hieroglyphics, formulates answers in the alphabet of destiny.

Cowrie Seashells

Of special note within the offerings is the cowrie seashell. Scientifically known as the *Cyprea maneta*, they're typically gathered in the West African Coast. Banished from the depths of the sea, unraveling like the immensities of our subconscious, they're the link to our own inner divinity like a tiny spark from our spiritual guides.

The acoustically silent sea reveals an audible sound on land of the Orishás, creating sentences by putting in conjunction all the forces of Nature, summoning and highlighting them in each invocation and request.

They are also popularly known in Spanish as *cauris* and particularly in Brazil as *búzios*. Initially they were used for the ancient Yoruba as currency in trade. They not only served as a measure of monetary value but formed and still form an important part of all the rituals and religious ceremonies of their village as well as the design and making of their jewels, items of daily use, clothing, and artwork.

In the Yoruban culture, we can observe a greater uptake of the magic-religious world through its works of art where the cowrie usually excels. We could say that no activity escapes the use of these seashells. They're the immutable, but at the same time experiential, witnesses of all religious and philosophical cultural manifestations.

1: Divination in Other Cultures

Throughout history, Humanity has experienced a captivating attraction to the fascinating power of *mancias* (divination) exerted by humankind. And, as Cicero said at the beginning of his *Treatise on Divination*, divination is a very ancient belief and is not limited to only a few people, whether they are enlightened, wise, or are from nations without a high level of development, since it does not depend on their cultural level. It ensures that there are faculties or inclinations for divination in humans. It's impossible to reject the idea that in some of them there is the power of prediction. It is also considered the potential factor by which humans can approach Divinity.

Divination in the
Old Greco-Roman Civilization

The Romans inherited an affection for the oracle systems of the Greeks, who called divination *mantique*. They connected it with Divinity, merged it into many of their concepts and principles, and were a carrier of true access to the divine world. This was called *divinatio*.

This term further reveals a spiritual need of the peoples who are more religious or who have a greater inner urgency for everything spiritual, considering not only the origin but also the end of human existence in need of contact with spheres beyond their daily routine and relative to the material area of existence.

The Romans absorbed religious structures from the Greeks. The Hellenic influence was reflected in Cumae (south of Naples) where the center of the oracle worship of the Sibyl was located. They were based on the books of the Sibyl, which for more than four centuries were hidden in the capital until they were transferred to the new Augustal del Palatino temple made in marble, built by Augusto and dedicated to Latona, Diana, and Apollo.

The prophecies with which the Sibylline books were created served as consultation for pontiffs and monarchs that on several occasions sent delegates to the oracle of Delphi. Sharing these beliefs is also based on the observation of natural phenomena believing in the word of the *augurs* (ancient Roman officials charged with observing and interpreting omens for guidance in public affairs) as well as foreseeing through the *auspices* (coming from the word "auspex," which means fortune-teller.)

Evidence of active divinatory activity is found in famous works such as *Oedipus* by Sophocles, where politics, the civil world, and society are intermingled with divinities, oracles, and diviners.

Apollo brings revelation; his voice is heard from Olympus and his answer falls in the oracle of Delphi. From there, the present, past, and future are simple pieces of chess that are moved by circumstances and invisible events. In works like the *Iliad* and the *Odyssey*, similar situations describe a development in which communication with the Divine puts a finishing touch on the expression of these manifestations.

Even in times when philosophical currents adverse to divination and cults ruled, these arts were prevalent in communities, their leaders, and their armies, as in their best times of abundance. The word *mantiké* represented the almost maniacal furor for divination done by Pythias, Bacchides, and/or Sibyls. These ancient pythonesses work in an extreme sense of deep mystical state and celestial ecstasy and are directly inspired by their connection with the supernatural. For Plato, this form was the purest, perhaps more irrational in its methods, and in turn, the most divine in its essence.

There is another way of understanding which is based on the observation of different phenomena such as the flight of birds, the study of their anatomy (especially the liver), birds singing, stargazing, moon eclipses, or even the observation of fish as it was done in Syria or Lycia (modern day Turkey).

The first of these forms worked naturally and only needed an operator and the divinity. The second needed agents bearing the divine message, their signs, and the ability to interpret them. In this way the Greeks and Romans consulted the oracles and believed that the gods could predict their future. The oracles were instructive, sharply imparting their designs.

History shows us the great value that enhanced the interpretation of the messages given by the pythonesses, since success depended not only on the configuration of the messages but also on the form of breaking up and interpreting the advice, because in most cases it could be ambiguous or confusing.

Foolishness or impulsiveness while deciphering the phrases could lead to big disappointments. Questions were answered in the form of judgments or verdicts, as when the king of Lydia, Croesus, asked the oracle about his fate in the battle against Cyrus. The answer is commonly translated as "Yes, Croesus will make war and destroy a great empire." And in fact it was so, only that the great empire destroyed was that of the king of Lydia and not of the Persians. The oracle had not been wrong, only the interpretation was incorrect.

Two oracles competed in importance: the one consecrated to Zeus in Dodona de Epirus, and that of Apollo in Delphi, a city sheltered between mountains and in close contact with nature.

At the foot of Mount Parnassus was perhaps the most important of the oracles: Delphi. There, the answers were attributed to Apollo, son of Leto and Zeus, known also as Delphic Apollo for being born in Delos.

The "King of the Day," "Phoebus," or "Radiant" was the owner of the light and had countless divine attributes. Just like Artemis (his sister), he appeared in many representations carrying a bow and an arrow, or in other cases a lyre as he also ruled the arts, especially music, and letters.

Gold letters appeared on the entrance walls to the temple, forming phrases like "Know thyself," "Beware of exaggeration," and "Live simply," attributed to the seven sages of Greece, deep insiders of astrology, geography, mathematics, and other sciences.

Throughout a myth, Delphi took on the character of Center of the World. Delphi tells that Zeus (Supreme Head of Olympus) left two eagles free from places separated by long distance to discover and meet one another in the center of the world. Both birds arrived at Delphi where there was a huge stone called *omphalos* (meaning navel), guarded by a great snake: Python.

After killing the monstrous animal, Apollo founded his earthly abode there. This became one of the most crowded oracles where the Pythia or Pythoness (from the term Python) sat opposite to an emanation of cold air and vapors (*pneüma*) on top of a gold tripod to answer questions and behind large veils separating them from the priests, who were the only ones who could approach them.

Those attending the temple were to perform conciliatory rites considered unavoidable for the intended purpose. Pursuing their purification, they bathed in the pure waters of the Castalia fountain and then made offerings.

And the responses came with an abrupt and sometimes crazy frenzy to which the priests quickly and practically tried to transcribe at times in rhyme or in quick, short phrases. The wisest and most experienced ones transcribed the questions with their respective answers on small wooden boards that over time were forming a true record of consultants.

The doubts and resolutions from the oracle acted as an archive, advising a possible reformulation of identical or similar cases or situations. The so-called official interpreters acted as real poets putting together strange messages of the god Apollo that did not always arrive with the clarity required.

The deity spoke through the mouths of the Pythias as a medium (in full state of possession), of moral norms, social, philosophical, or state issues and politics in general.

Other priests, the Selloi (belonging to Dodona) received their prophecies from the oracle of Zeus. These Nordic priests aimed more at the rituals of purification together with meditation practices. To hear the prophecies, they fulfilled rituals of burning herbs and plants that induced and appeased the different trances that crossed the Pythonesses.

Divinatory and especially inspiring power was awarded to the nymphs and the Muses where the Nereids, the daughters of Doris and Nereus (possessor of the gift of the prophecy), formed the fifty nymphs of the sea.

The system of oracles was not only used as a mode of prediction; it also served for other purposes such as in the Temple of Asclepius. While they slept, the sick people who went to the temple received divine messages where not only the deity communicated what type of disease attacked the affected, but also prescribed different cures.

The healing by divine intermediation was also present in ancient magical thinking where the oracles fulfilled the function of seeing the future and were integrated into a complex religious dynamism.

Humans went their way over the centuries. They faced their fears, some overcame them and others still remain as remnants of old mental structures and social conditions that anchor and lock. These structures make humans falter and often doubt our own psychic properties. They make them move away from the God–Man connection, and in the worst case, turn into a materialistic being.

While it is true that the gifts of precognition are not for everyone (because they are a divine gift to the chosen ones), intuition, development of mental capacities, and training in different divination techniques are general tools within the reach of humanity.

Divination in Christianity

Returning to take into account certain antecedents, we will see that in the best-selling book in the world (considered as sacred by the majority), we get some interesting facts. Let's look together at some of this revealing data.

Perhaps one of the greatest messages from the Beyond to Humankind, are those found in the form of spiritual communication in the Sacred Bible.

This communication constitutes irrefutable proof of esoteric sources that demonstrate messages and revelations. For example, the Holy Gospel according to St. Matthew, Chapter 1, says that an angel of the lord appeared to Joseph through dreams communicating the arrival of his son conceived by the work and grace of the Holy Spirit. Joseph, son of David, was not afraid to receive this order and called the child with the name of Jesus because, according to revelation, he would save men and their people from their sins (Matthew 18, 20, and 21).

Syncretism of Christianity and the Orishás

Due to the fact that slavery was common in the Americas, men and women of color were forced to worship their saints secretly and carefully.

They were harassed and forced to accept a faith they did not understand, while missing their Orishás more and more. They acquired strength from thinking about them and hoping to rescue their values as an ethnic group. Despite the prohibitions imposed by their enslavers, they went on venerating their Orishás by hiding them behind the images of Roman Catholic saints, or on shelves below them, concealed by embroidered altar clothes.

Thus they compared saints to Orishás, like the fighting strength of Ogún with St. George or St. Anthony, etc., until they were able to draw a true parallelism between their faith, their conceptions, and the beliefs of the white man.

Many Africans are opposed to syncretism, and there are also Christians who are disturbed by the comparison.

I do not consider syncretism a misguided or illogical theory because, as we have seen, at the beginning it was a need, and now all those values are embedded and interpenetrated in the mechanisms of faith. I believe this is a form of comparatively universal thinking. Syncretism forms a new faith similar if not equal to the original and provides a means of acceptance. It is enriching because it includes new sociocultural ingredients and spices. It adapts to the modes of a new land and age and contributes to the fraternization of cultures.

Syncretism is a deeply emotional subject throughout the Americas, and whether accepted or rejected, the fact is that it exists. More than that, it would seem that the more it is ignored or denied, the stronger it becomes—perhaps an echo of the reaction of past prohibitions.

Humanity has always searched for and idealized its conceptions: admired bravery, beauty, and justice, and tried to absorb them, to materialize them. Many times they were sought in popular idols from different branches of the arts, politics, or other places. The search extended to the religious world and philosophical trends that paid greater attention to inner, moral, and/or spiritual concerns. This has occurred from time immemorial and continues to occur.

In ancient civilizations such as the Greco-Roman, syncretism was used extensively to explain origins, conquests, defeats, and so on. My intention now is to make a comparison with them and—this should be very clear—not to create a new syncretism. Although there are similarities in some cases, there are also marked differences even in those cases.

We shall therefore carry out a conceptual comparison among symbolisms, origins, and spheres of action, leaving other aspects aside.

Note that more than one Roman Catholic saint corresponds to the same Orishá; this is due to the fact that many African nations settled in America. Each of them chose different representations according to their own context and the strength of the prevailing saint or the saint most cherished by their white masters.

But as an old, very dear, and much respected black man once told me, "It is necessary that they come to you and know you not only for your name, but for what you are and represent..."

Catholic Saints	Orishás
Saint Anthony, The Holy Child of Atocha, Saint Joseph, Saint Peter	Elegguá
Saint George, Saint Peter, Saint John, Saint Anthony	Ogún or Ogúm
Saint George	Ochosi or Oxossi
Saint Barbara, Saint Teresa, Saint Joan of Arc	Iansá or Oyá
Saint Catherine, Saint Rita, Virgin of Carmen	Obá
Saint John the Baptist, Saint Mark of Leon, Archangel Michael, Saint Barbara	Changó or Xangó
Saint Lazarus, Saint Roch	Babaluallé, Xapaná
Our Lord Jesus Christ	Obaluaié or Omulú
Saint Joseph, Saint Benedict, Saint Sebastian	Osain
Saint Cosmas, Saint Damian	Ibeyis
Saint Christopher, Saint Michael the Archangel	Aggayú Solá
Saint John the Baptist	Osún
Virgin of the Charity of the Copper, Immaculate Conception, Virgin Mary	Ochún or Oxúm
Saint Bartholomew	Oshumaré
Our Lady of Candelas, Our Lady of Rule, and Stella Maris	Iemanjá or Yemayá
Our Lady of the Rosary	Dadá
Saint Clare	Yewa

Catholic Saints	Orishás
Our Lady of Carmen, Saint Ana	Naná Burukú
Saint Francis of Assisi	Orunlá
Holy Spirit	Ifá
Sacred Heart of Jesus, Our Lady of Mercedes, Senhor do Bonfim (Lord of Good End), Jesus of Nazareth	Oxalá, Orixalá, Obatalá

We have spoken of the Greeks and Romans as historical examples of two great civilizations, then of Christianity as an example of a major religion. But in reality, as we said at the beginning, all the peoples throughout their existence have turned to divination. People thought that this was the divine tool, which the Creator had given us, and that established through invisible threads the communication with the Hereafter. All this until today, in the twenty-first century, was the future and hope of tomorrow. But there are many who do not yet dare to look at the heavens, perhaps as a sign of internal shame.

But God, in his infinite wisdom, fills the eyes of stars of those who dare to look beyond. He renews their faith, gives them courage, and leaves faith and hope in their souls.

2: The Yoruba and Santería

Yoruba Civilization and Religion

This culture took advantage of its technical development without forgetting the foundations that connected it with the spiritual. This was perhaps one of the most present premises throughout of all its development as a civilization.

In an anthropological context, this society would be defined as Animist. (Although I personally don't like the idea of boxing or delineating high cultures with such particular definitions, labeling them in some way.) They began an active trade based on the sale and commercialization of exquisite works of art made from different metals.

From this data we can appreciate its high sociocultural value. The performance in these activities reflects their intellectual content. Of course, its artistic value will always be manifested in a very clear trend and expectation: religious and spiritual transcendence. Religion was the soul of this high people and also the basis of this hierarchical civilization.

The way of interpreting and facing life was based on spiritual knowledge. Nothing transcended beyond and nothing could happen that escaped these domains. The soul handled everything and all things depended on a mother soul. The power of faith's full conviction was the carving weapon, perpetual and never hesitant of its civilization.

Art and religious conceptions were and are the same and everything revolved around them. Sculptural works in metals, wood, stone, jewels (bracelets, rings, and necklaces), as well as sticks and scepters were conceived and created from a revealing mysticism.

Their religious emblems were seen in knives, spears, and swords and also in splendid ivory carvings, embossed in leather and works on canvas. All works profiled toward the search and perpetuity of a concept that seemed universal: the immortality of the soul.

In all these embodiments, the use of the cowrie rarely escaped, either as measure of value or when they were already consecrated as bastions of power or as representatives of mystical fighting forces that would defend their possessors from attacks. In this way, the seashell was the language of the Deities in their social and cultural life.

Their religion, based on a complex system of trade-offs between the cosmos, nature, and the individual, represents both the simplest adaptation of man and the existential wheel of life. Divination has always formed a very important part within the religious jurisdiction.

We could define it as evidently magical, powerful, enthralling, subjugating, mystical par excellence. It opens the portals for spiritual communication awakening the latent powers in Humankind and the indispensable tools for our evolution.

The Yorubas believed in supernatural beings, powerful and sacred, of a great first cause. The beings, which they called the Orishás, pure energies of light, collaborated from the beginning with the designs of Almighty God, to which they called Olorum—a flashing, formless energy being, omnipresent, omnipotent, and omniscient.

Olodumaré was another of God's names, "the beginning without end," the beginning of beginnings, Creator of the Universe and of all living things therein found, ruled the Orún (the other World) controlling the precepts of eternity without end.

God, so distant to the conception of the human mind, was present in faith and feeling through the culture of the Orishás, also known as Orichás or Orixás, who live and dwell in all of nature (in the sea, the wind, lightning, thunder, rock, stones, rain, lakes, waterfalls, rivers, plants, trees, etc.).

Each of them has influence on human qualities by highlighting and reinforcing them. Thus came the voice of thunder in the figure of Shangó, regent of the Supreme Justice. Or the femininity of Oshún in all freshwater's currents, the deity of love, the Aphrodite of the Yoruba Pantheon. They recognized the protective gifts of Mother Nature, incorporating her as and essential factor in all links of life, respected her and considered her as the great mother.

Its philosophical conception lies in the belief that all things are alive—even those apparently inert, immobile, or however low their vibratory frequency. Even in them there is life, perhaps in a later stage of evolution, slow or imperceptible. It all forms part of a general energy consensus that will report its actions and its development in this world at the precise and necessary moment before the Creator.

The Yorubas believed in two universal and just laws: the Law of Karma and the Law of Reincarnation. They cradled their civilization under these concepts, trying to overcome earthly difficulties without forgetting the spirit (the maker of all things, the motor of the body, living essence itself.) They had to take care of this spirit, intending to make its stay in this World as "correct" as possible by trying to increase their good actions and eliminating errors of previous lives.

In order for their spirits to vibrate again in unison in the creative light, reaching in this way their total evolution, they did not fear eternal punishments nor did they believe in a devastating hell, because they knew that humans impose punishments on themselves.

God simply allows us to use the greater human condition: free will, and through it, the exercise of our own individual freedom. In this way they conceptualized life respecting nature, working for the improvement of one's soul, venerating and considering with utmost respect one's elders and ancestors and raising children from the time they are little under mystical and esoteric concepts so that the magical conception of things was as natural as the fact of breathing, necessary and uncontrollably autonomous.

The Yoruba Religion in America

This religion came to be established by one of the most inhuman forms of submission: slavery, the most aberrant and incomprehensible action that any mind can imagine, the most defiant of the low passions, the worst of feelings and perhaps the most serious fault for the human soul.

Slavery took on new strength in America, relying mostly on ancient and painful legal antecedents. Around the fifteenth century, Spain and Portugal had an expansionist policy based on slave interests. The Azores and the Canary Islands became the nexus between Africa and the Iberian Peninsula, increasing the continuity of ship traffic between those destinations.

Being that slavery was a lot more interesting than the existing and intensive trade based on gold, other metals, and grains, there were several reasons for its upsurge. These include:

a. The requests made by people of great importance and political weight
b. The new councils established in the new continent
c. The need for free labor for the gold and copper mines as well as for cotton, sugar, and other plantations.

It also established the belief that the work of black men was more productive than that of Native Americans because it yielded much more and tired much less. Another of the so-called causes was the system of royalties and exceptions enjoyed by the majority of expedition leaders and their commanders. They were also exempted by the King of Spain and the Council of the Indies from paying taxes for the entry of personal slaves that increased the trafficking even more.

Officials (including governors, viceroys, religious, and/or parish managers) could not sell their slaves. In reality, the prohibition was rarely followed and mini slave markets were created in distant areas.

Another of the franchises that contributed was the inability to release the black slaves. These factors, along with others of a social and economic order, increased this system. In the beginning, the epicenter of expansionist activity was established in the Antilles. From there, the threads of a new economic structure were handled, giving way to a sentiment of slavery. The population of indigenous people—Native Americans—was diminishing with the passage of time, making more and more necessary a greater recruitment of labor. Therefore, the large-scale importation of black slaves occurred in an explosive and unsustainable manner.

It was done in two different ways: directly from Africa to the Americas, or from distribution centers to specific consumer markets. Even if there was a greater work structure, it didn't mean there was a tax or customs system.

Despite these controls that served as the basis for current statistics, they performed a meticulous contraband trade that made it impossible to know with accuracy the number of ships, nor the number of slaves. Ports such as Havana, Cartagena, and Veracruz were the most used to unload slaves in the Americas. There were also frequent stops in the Canary Islands for provisions. The areas of Africa that were looted expanded from the North of the continent to the southern part depended on its extraction focus.

According to the origin of the Spanish authorities, the slaves were classified as:

a.   Slaves of the Levant, possessors of a great Islamic influence coming from the area of Mauritania

b. Slaves of the rivers of Guinea, the area of the same name or Cape

c. Verde, much appreciated by Dutch, Portuguese, and British

d. Slaves from Sierra Leone, who came from south of the area formerly belonging to the Gold Coast

e. Slaves of the region of Angola, denominated "Casta Angola," also known as Loandas, Benguelas, and other names

f. Slaves from the region known as Portuguese India, east coast of Africa, the Philippines, Malay Archipelago, and Indian regions

g. Slaves from Mozambique and Bantu (Cafre)

h. Slaves from Congo

i. Slaves from Sao Tome

j. Slaves from Terra Nova

k. Slaves from Novos (from the islands of Sao Tome, areas of Congo and Cameroon)

The slaves were denigrated and transported like animals without respecting their human condition. Men of infinite wisdom were shipped in a cruel and irreverent way. Fighters, tireless warriors, exquisite artists, and powerful priests were stacked almost with the same conceptualization as objects.

Slave traders did not care about their souls, their ideas, or their dreams. They had no right to anything, not even to their own lives, and were in the hands of the enslavers. Slaves meant money that produced work and progress for their owners. The younger and stronger were more desirable because they would produce more and eat and sleep less. They would also endure more the inclemency of the weather, the whipping and the abusive punishments.

Their cries of helplessness drowned in their throats as the whip marked the skin tanned by the sun. In their sad looks and in their hearts was the faith in their Orishás and in the conviction that this great nightmare would end.

And so it was. Their spiritual forces and guides did not abandon them at any time. They responded to each of their requests and to each of their pleas. And with the patience and resignation that only wisdom brings, they worked with hope and kindness toward their brothers.

And despite the prohibitions imposed by their masters, they continued to cultivate their Deities by camouflaging them with a religious syncretism, rich in comparisons and powerful in their conceptions as the only viable means to continue their religious practices. The evangelization helped them discover the doctrinal elements that served to adapt their forces required for the new cult.

Syncretism was changing throughout the Americas because of the popularity of the Catholic saints reigning in the different areas. And so the slave began a long pilgrimage where the faith in his Orishás was gaining respect for what they called *Santos*, making the usual comparisons.

With all this doctrinal-religious background, the first fortune-tellers who disembarked in America were promptly teaching their followers the ancestral knowledge of infinite wisdom about precognition and the different puzzles of Destiny.

The Importance of Magic Symbols, Constellations, and Nature in Mystical Revelations

Three Wise Men from the East arrived in Jerusalem in the time of King Herod. They were asking where the recently born King of the Jews was. "Because we have his star in the East and we come to worship him" (Mateo 2:2). They were seeking the child who would become the most powerful and the most humble of Kings.

The most important priests and scribes of the town were convening by Herod. Those who claimed that he would be born in Bethlehem of Judea, said it was "written" by the prophet.

Then Herod, secretly calling the wise men, inquired of them diligently the time of the appearance of the star. He asked them that once they find their location, they would notify him in a hurry because he too would love the child. The star guided the wise men, marking the path ahead and stopping where Jesus was. "And when they saw the star, they rejoiced with exceedingly great joy" (Mateo 2:10).

When they saw the child next to Mary, they knelt and worshiped him and offered him three magic gifts: gold, myrrh, and incense. But their dreams prophesied that they would not reveal to Herod their finding and returned to their land by another path.

After their departure, Joseph again had contact with an angel through dreams who told him, "Get up and take the child and his mother and flee to Egypt and remain there until I tell you, because it will happen that Herod will seek the child to kill him" (Mateo 2:13). And he did so fleeing to Egypt.

There he was in that magical land until he knew that Herod had died "to fulfill what the Lord said through the prophet when he said: 'From Egypt I called my Son'" (Mateo 2:15). Herod ordered to kill all children under two years old that were in Bethlehem and the surrounding areas, according to the times calculated by the wise men.

Once again, the prophecy and the voice of a prophet in this case were fulfilled. So Jeremiah said, "A voice was heard in Ramah, great lamentation, weeping and groaning, Rachel weeping at her children and did not want to be comforted because they perished" (Mateo 2:18).

At other times, the angel's message is received and understood by Joseph through divination in dreams, being already in Egypt. And then he, "advised by revelation in dreams, went to the region of Galilee" (Mateo 2:22). Coming to the region of Nazareth "that it might be fulfilled which was spoken by the prophets who were to be called Nazarene" (Mateo 2:23).

Who would doubt or call into question the divinatory value of the star belonging to the constellation of Cassiopeia that guided Melchior, Caspar, and Balthazar? No one can deny the clairvoyant accuracy of the great biblical prophets or the dream messages of the angels of God.

With respect to the latter, St. Thomas Aquinas would reaffirm it, recognizing the veracity and lawful character of dream divination or oneiromancy. In the work *Summa Theologica,* he wrote that God reveals his desires to Humankind. In the Old Testament we find the custom that Hebrew people had to consult the Lord through the use of Urim and Thummin, which is essentially the casting or drawing of lots. Similarly, consultations were used with people who could communicate with the spirit world, having premonitory and revealing visions using a symbolism rich in metaphorical expressions.

In Israel, the soothsayers were known by the name of *Nabhi* (the called beings), inspired by the Divine breath. Great prophets like Isaiah, Jeremiah, Ezekiel, Micah, Zephaniah, Hosea, Elisha, Elias and others fill pages loaded with mysticism, some of which predicted the Babylonian invasion, the devastation of Judah, among many other verifiable facts.

Therefore, we see in different cultures how the need to contact Divinity through emissaries, different characters, angels, diviners, prophets, or mediums, directly or indirectly, always prevailed. Humankind did not want to feel alone, and in the need to be accompanied, they sought the infinite protection of being recognized and accepted through different spiritual communications, obtaining the necessary answers to the difficulties that life itself imposed.

And those answers came, no matter how, with what voices, with what means, or in what form. The truth is that they arrived, and in doing so, it felt that creation was improving. And from the black continent came first to America and then the rest of the World, the most magical tool of a civilization that we already mentioned, the Yoruba.

This tool, the peaceful weapon of free souls was, and it is, divination. It became the center and guiding linchpin of a culture and a philosophy. Throughout the Americas and as a form of unification, it is known as *Santería,* or the philosophical-religious lineage that brings together all these concepts.

Divination in Santería

Divination came to America as it was practiced in Africa, but now takes on the name of Santería ("worship of Saints," or Orishás). It's as rich and extensive as it is complex. It is as wide and varied as all of nature, because it was also part of the belief of the ancient African that in every creative act of Divinity there was a breath of life and a hidden message that humans should reveal. The undisputed stamp, the most outstanding paragon inside it, is called a "letter," or *meji* (see appendix for their illustrations). But what does a meji represent?

The action named "record of a letter" compromises the determination of an *Odú* or *Ordún,* each of the different readings and/or throws that are determined in Ifá or in the Diloggún, and in doing so consistently arises the verbalization of sayings and the most fantastic legends, some of which have been converted into the greatest myths of the stories of the Orishás. These comprise a foundation of our divination in this book.

Phrases and short sentences will assert with great certainty the future of the consultant, and the causes that provoked it will be told in each one of the Odús. Each story brings learning and experience, and each wise teaching foretells of good fortune or the dangers that lie in waiting.

The Orishás appear, unfolding within their pantheon with enormous mystical power, and together with other important characters, they reveal tales that will exemplify in a simple but deep way the Odús of *Diloggún,* the act of using consecrated cowrie seashells as a means of divination. It is an abbreviation for the term Merindiloggún.

Each of these signs recognizes one or several important stories called *patakkíes,* stories of legends and myths relating to the Orishás, which emphasize the human virtues, tending to them and always leaving a teaching, an opinion, for our conscience and making us reconsider even the simplest examples.

In a sobering and magical way, the Saints or Orishás share the scene of action with common men, rulers, inanimate beings, plants, animals.

Everything comes alive. The power of Animism increases and takes indescribably rich meaning.

The priest, an experienced diver in the art of deepening and venturing to describe the destiny of people, will speak in his stories with extra caution and will impose on his words an unmistakable ceremonial touch. He'll have the difficult but not impossible mission to remember the necessary patakkí without getting them confused. He'll know that he has the responsibility of accurately transmitting nothing more and nothing less than many of the stories of the Orishás.

Either extravagantly or not, in some cases with greater synchronicity and sometimes with more rich expression, you should always respect every sign because they all speak for themselves as they represent the ancient knowledge and wisdom of their ancestors.

The person who consults the seashells will not only listen to the description of the story, but also how to save themselves from possible danger in the future, current dangers, or how to increase or ensure their happiness or wellness.

The Deities of the Yoruba Pantheon speak through the seashells and only the priest prepared for such purposes may interpret in the manner structured by religious canons. No other person can handle the consecrated seashells, as it would not only cause serious misconduct, but they also would not be empowered to do so, not having the *Ashé*, or the strength, grace, or power, also pronounced and/or written as Axé or Aché, necessary and therefore wouldn't get a true answer.

Ashé is not bought. You'll get it with many years of training and learning, with great humility and sacrifice. In ancient Africa, from a child's birth onward, Oracles were consulted to reveal the child's future and how they would perform in society. Only some of them were chosen as fortune-tellers and only a few were ordained over time as priests. The Deities responded and they chose according to the destiny of each child. Even among the priests, there were different occupations according to the Orishá assigned to their heads. There were healers, herbalists, those who prepared all the magical-religious ornaments, and so forth.

The prepared priest, the true priest, knows that every reading puts into motion a sacred and not profane mechanism. Be aware that this is the bridge and mediator for a short time between this real and tangible world and the other distant world that is actually invisible, but just as real and true as the tangible one. That is why he prepares himself to fulfill his role worthily by studying, analyzing, deepening the teachings received from his elders, and trying to get all the material needed to keep his conscience clean to avoid loosing his true Ashé.

For these purposes, his vibrational and spiritual field is very important. His preservation allows you to venture into the field of paranormal demonstrations using invocations, prayers, and requests that get closer and connect with the divine inner spark with his Orishá ruler. At the end, this relationship reaches its maximum expression when this process is linked with the Divine.

Generally, a certain amount of money stipulated by the trades is paid to the soothsayer, something fair and deserved, if we consider that that's their job, their time, and their profession. But also as goes the very popular saying among Santeros: "Who lives for the altar, shall live from the altar." As in any other religion, the parishioner will cooperate and help monetarily in their search for magic help to solve their problems, whether material, sentimental, spiritual, or others.

It's necessary to clarify that the priest is morally and religiously obliged to those who do not really have the financial resources to pay for their record, also to those who cannot afford the materials needed to perform any indicated ebó, or offerings and magical work. The true priest knows that the real reward is found in other worlds of existence, in other planes, and that there's a compensation law that covers and protects him.

This law is universal and correlated with the law of Karma. That's to say, it rules for all and therefore the consultants must be honest and sincere and not gamble with these situations, perhaps depriving other people who really do not have the means to pay for their visit or carry out spiritual cleansing.

It is important to bear in mind that in the different avatars of the world of magic, it's known that always, and in a representative manner in these cases, it's good to leave at least a penny, and thus symbolically we will have fulfilled our task.

The Orishás will certainly give you later on the opportunity to buy a bouquet of flowers, an oil lamp for several days, or any other small present that shows your gratitude for the Holy Quarter (sacred place where the Santero has the settlement or the home of his saints). No matter how small the offering may be, the saints will receive it with the same love and with the same gratitude of a greater gift. Keep in mind that in the field of the spiritual, feelings prevail.

Actually, the right or payment for your consult is always little if we consider that, metaphorically speaking, once the call to the Orishás takes place, the journey, more extraordinary than any mind can imagine between the Beyond and our dimension, will begin.

Main Attributes of the Orishás Who Were Most Worshipped

Each of the Orishás has a special attribute, a certain *Ashé* (grace or power) by which it exerts its power, action, or will. They collaborate with the will of the Sovereign, of God Almighty. Being reflections of God's infinite Wisdom and Intelligence, they represent the irrefutable and necessary links in the representative chain of the spiritual evolution of Humanity.

It could be said that all the interconnected mechanisms of life in this world are due to the generative action of the Orishás. In a sense, Orishás are nature itself, while humankind is the most important component of the animal kingdom. Because humans are one of the most necessary steps in the evolutionary wheel, they have a spiritual fusion with the Orishás that goes beyond rational thought.

Hence the Orishás are their guardian angels and spiritual custodians who deal with complex mechanisms such as the one represented by the spirit-mind-brain connection to accompany them in their lives as beings embodied here on Earth. But their attributes not only concentrate on the spiritual; they also have an influence on material life by tending and helping so that humans can correct and solve their physical and/or material needs. It's recognized as a premise that a body well cared for, healthy, free of vices, diseases, and dangers, is the perfect place to accommodate the spirit.

In this way, the soul or spirit of human beings can fulfill a universal and superior law: the Law of Reincarnation, for it is overcoming, spiritually evolving, and repairing past errors and faults committed in other lives here on this planet.

Each of the Orishás represents a virtue, gift, or quality and provides protection that exalts a special feeling. It also marks in their spiritual or protected children a psychological archetype and gives them a type of physical structure. Often it's very simple for the good observer or a religious person with experience to determine the spiritual guides of someone according to the traits of the face, musculature, the body structure, and moral and spiritual conducts.

In these cases, depending on experience or good judgment, there is no completely certain answer. When you want to determine the Orishás corresponding to a person, namely the Orishá guide, rector of his head, or commonly known as Guardian Angel, the Orishás are those who decide by means of the consecrated shells.

The elements of Nature are under the Orishá's orders. They have one or several plants, flowers, trees, etc. where they base their Ashé and they're also represented by stones and natural products such as honey used in rituals and offerings pertaining to Oshún.

In this way, Elegguá becomes the careful and loyal vigilante, protector and guardian of all doors and entrances to houses, shops, villages, towns, and cities. He is the specialist in opening doors in relation to jobs, careers or professions.

Ogún and Oshossi, the brave warriors, symbolically fight with their swords, bows, and arrows against all forms of wickedness, witchcraft, or any other form of spiritual submission.

Iansá or Oyá, the deity of the winds and possessor of the beam given by her husband Shangó, wins in any difficult contest and in matters where others find it hard to penetrate, like the holy fields, where with her *Iruexim* she directs and controls the souls. An Iruexim is a feather duster made by Babaluallé or Omulú horse manes to seek healing, receive physical relief, reduce pain, stop wounds, comfort the body, etc.

In order to solve the most complicated cases of love, Obá transforms into a suffering, self-sacrificing lover.

Shangó is the champion of Divine Justice to solve lawsuits, judgments, formalities, paperwork, etc., or simply to shelter under his righteous robe.

Osain owns all leaves, herbs, flowers, and plants. He knows all the secrets and powers of each part and each of the components of the vegetable kingdom.

Ibeyi protects children until they reach adolescence, also to those who rescue the innocence and simplicity by highlighting high human values.

Aggayú Solá is the protector of drivers and walkers.

Osún is part of the quartet of the so-called warriors of Santería (along with Elegguá, Oshossi, and Ogún.) He is a faithful watchman, incorruptible and indefatigable in his task.

Oshún is the deity of love and represents sweetness.

Yemayá is the protective mother and the custodian of homes.

Oxalá or Obatalá, the sovereign father, is just, a redeemer, maker of peace and love.

Each one of them fulfills their strenuous mission, trying to transmute pain into joy and happiness so that humanity can fulfill its passage of incarnation so that in a time not so distant, all the souls will vibrate to the unison of perfection and in complete harmony with the Creator.

3: Ifá

Presence of Ifá

The manifestation of Ifá is present through his words (Ofó), which in turn are made up of legends, myths, or stories (Odús) and by previous invocations and prayers with power (Ashé) that pronounces the Awo Ifá (Teacher or foreseer of Ifá) to link and communicate the world of the Deities and spirits to the world of humans.

The representation of Ifá in the Earth is limited to the sacred space delimited by the Opón de Ifá or when the Merindiloggún is used by the magic circle formed by the different collars that are arranged on the table, mat, or cloth where the priest implores and transcends with his word, anointing between the Faith and his voice. Ifá will be present through the different vehicles to transmit his Wisdom. The fortune-teller recites, when necessary the "Ese" (verses) corresponding to the beginning of the reading during the different rituals or when required by his psychic receptor apparatus to be able to keep in medium-psychic contact with the Divinity.

While in reading with four pieces of Obí, it is only necessary to be initiated because the response involved the ancestors that are usually part of the consultant's personal universe, it is different when the sixteen Ikines are manipulated or handled because they enter the system of Dafa. In this case, it is essential that the person doing the reading be a priest dedicated to Ifá and considered within the priestly rank as having a higher level than Babalocha or Babalorishá who generally consults the cowries in numbers of four, eight, or sixteen shells.

Both the systems of divination by Ikines or by means of Opelé are reserved for the men who hold the title of Awo (foreseers) or Babalawos (Parents of the secret.) However, the woman also occupies an important position in worship to Ifá, receiving the denomination of *Apetebí*, that initially in Africa were generally the women of the fortune-tellers.

Initially women also had this restriction to consult with seashells. Those who could perform this function had to have Oshún Yabá Omí as Orishá, ruler of her head, the most ancestral of all the Oshún types, and being Apetebís, they acted as priests next to the Babalawo.

Today the priestesses and priests can consult the Diloggún when working with seashells. One of the stories about the role of women as an active part in the process of divination tells us about the time when Yemayá, being married to Orulá, achieved fame as a diviner in the absence of her husband. When Orulá was busy visiting other lands where his services were required, Yemayá finds herself under a moral obligation to attend to the insistent requests of her husband's former patients. After a time of coexistence with Orulá, and due to her sensitivity and humanitarian gifts, her ability developed with the Oracle, and the queen of the Oceans turned into a great fortune-teller.

Despite the fact that Yemayá repeatedly refused to venture into Orulá's delicate work, people crowded and waited for long hours behind her door. After attending the first client, she could not rest or refuse. Her prestige was traveling throughout all the villages until her fame reached the ears of Orulá who could not believe what was happening. When he could not accept what was being said, he returned home. When he reached his home, he saw a long line of people who seemed to come from far away, standing in front of the his place, waiting for hours and hours to receive their query through the mouth of the woman fortune-teller.

When Orulá entered the house, and without waiting for Yemayá to finish her work, he questioned her harshly. She tried to make him realize that she had never wanted to take his place, and even less to become a real fortune-teller. Orulá, completely offended, did not understand the situation and the discussion reached such an extreme that it ended in separation. The two agreed that after what happened it was best to take their own paths.

This legend exemplifies the preponderant role that man has in Ifá. Hierarchically, they follow the Babalawo in the worship of Ifá, the Oluwo whom all obey, and the Odoffin and the Aró respectively. In these hierarchies one takes into account the position and fame of the soothsayers or assistants to initiate the prayers and invocations. The number of years of experience in both positions plays an important role.

The Ashé of Ifá

Ifá is expressed in the sky, in the air, and on the earth. His inspiring flight comprises the soul of the great visionaries and prophets inspired in all times and who, with extreme delicacy, can foresee events that go beyond materialistic structures.

Ifá imparts his knowledge to the wise in spirit, to those who have the mission of being able to interpret the designs of destiny that are unknowable labyrinths for the common of souls. Its reflective path implies the supreme knowledge of the being from its interior toward the outer spheres so that it can contemplate the things and extract its true essence. Only in this way will they be able to understand the events and reveal his symbols.

Its spectrum of vision is unlimited and timeless, but it can be translated into a comprehensible whole with a great power of understanding. In most iconographies, it is linked to birds, as in the various Ifá trays. The presence of these birds is almost always unalterable and relates them to the female forces and the Ying side existing in nature.

It is believed that Orumilá took the secrets of Ifá, thanks to his wife, characterizing Odú. His voice reaches the Earth after the fortune-teller, with his *Iroké Ifá* (divination tapper) in hand, hits the *Opón Ifá* (divination tray) where the *Irosun* (sacred dust) has already been sprayed on to make demarcations whose combinations configure the readings.

The Iroké Ifá, carved generally in ivory, is one of the indispensable elements for the work of the fortune-teller with which he requests the assistance of Orumilá, invoking him with gentle blows that rhythmically impacts the tip of the Iroké on the Opón in a careful and ceremonial way.

These rods measure between twenty to thirty centimeters long and have fine and exquisite ivory carvings that describe the religious passion and an elaborate mystical system. The represented images play a preponderant role.

Other materials such as wood, bronze, small pieces of glass, and beads of different colors put ceremonial rigor in the meaning of their implementation. The Iroké becomes a tool of true power, like a tiny baton of control, by which the Babalawo reorders energies propitiating each magical moment so that each force enters into action at the exact and required moment. It is like opening channels that would allow the penetration of the Ifá spirit in all these processes.

Its structure has three distinct parts that have to do with all the dynamics mentioned above.

The first part is located at its tip and does not have any engraving, and like the end that is refined in the shape of a nail or cone, it becomes more acute in the process of extrasensory perception. This part, called *Orí*, is the most sensorial of all because it is directly connected to the process of divination. Orí is the head of the Iroké and is intrinsically related to fate. Within this configuration are the *Orí Odé*, the visible conical part, and the *Orí Inú*, which means the "inner head." Orí Inú is the soul or essence that governs the behavior and personality of abstract thought and is invisible to the human eye.

The Orí Inú would be chosen beforehand by the human being before reincarnating so that he can accept the conditions of his Karma by committing his *Emí* (spirit) to lead his *Ara* (body) through secure terrain and to house a soul in healthy conditions, promising its care, respecting its life, and meeting the process of spiritual cleansing on Earth.

Here the Orí Inú regulates the psychic activity of people related to the mental processes of abstraction and thought. For this reason it is considered as the inner head, or the sacred part, and is placed hierarchically above the Orí Odé.

This action of prevailing, in a certain form of superiority, is called *Ayanmo* and represents the agreement between both parties to live together in harmony. This means: "What is bound in a fixed way to one."

This is the most effective part of the Iroké and the one that contains the mysteries of divination. It has its own life and autonomous capacities to direct, from its epicenter, the channeling of the inspiring forces—to capture the divine sparks revealing the presence of Orumilá.

The absence of images in the upper part is a great visual attraction and offers with more veracity the idea of something supernatural and mysterious at the same time. In the central part you can almost always see carvings of heads or female figures that when kneeling, in a position called *Ikunlé Abiyamo*, represent the uninterrupted cycles of eternal life. In spite of the existence of death as the momentary and palpable disappearance of this world, the ritual and artistic configuration of the mysteries of regeneration are taken into account, carrying in their womb the human potentials and giving life again in an interrupted way, connecting with the divine part, with the Orishás, that must be worshiped on the knees (*Akunlebo*) as a sign of respect and gratitude.

This greeting and reverence to the higher forces compromises the ideas of concentration and spiritual meditation in a moment of comforting ecstasy for your soul to feel supported and protected by the Divinities. The soul feels part of the whole universe, creation, and life without receiving any rejection. On the contrary, it reflects rapport and inclusion despite its human condition.

There is a belief that the woman (hence the number of female figures) has the ability to move the Deities by demonstrating fertility by giving birth. Pregnancy is the greatest proof of the prosperity that is sought. Her figure recreates the image of the continuity of the species, and therefore, who but she could appease the forces of nature?

In the final segment, before arriving at the base that is usually smooth and without carved drawings or only with some decorative guards, you can often see riders who would symbolize the wishes of believers to achieve dignified and successful positions in their lives with a relevant economic and social position.

In the *Agere Ifá*, (a kind of bowl with a base in the form of a foot and a lid), the priest of Ifá keeps the sixteen sacred walnuts from the palm tree where he converts the Ikines into sacred fruits and expression vehicles of Orumilá. The Agere can be of different sizes and are usually made of carved wood. There are very few in ivory. Most have almost theatrically staged performances of situations that encourage the anticipation of the desires of the consultants, such as prosperity, happiness, peace, balance, health, joy, and fellowship.

But undoubtedly, the greatest and most important tool of the fortune-teller, who also gives importance and social status, is his Iroke Ifá. It represents his status and social brilliance with which he becomes a priest with Iré Owo, a priest with wealth.

This conception may be due to the fact that in the past the ivory was very expensive and the tusk of elephant was designated only for the king and for others outstanding in their positions or functions. It was also for the high leaders and warrior men who defended the lands and possessions of the kingdom.

These are the tools that the fortune-teller uses to receive the Ashé of Orumilá. They always have a symbolic way of working within the world of magic and divination united in their poetic mysticism.

The fractioning of divination plots obey a neat visual image of contemplating the timelessness of divinatory magic with the times of mortals. This structure of thought is also reflected in the Opón Ifá, in the trays for divination, tables or trays of Ifá.

Etymologically, "Opón" means "the action of pleasing." For this reason they not only serve a divinatory purpose but are intended to please propitiating divinatory events through a good reception of all the forces that intervene, so that when combined they offer the expected result.

Yoruba devotion is present in the artistic designs and in the perfection of the lines, evoking situations that compromise their mystical-religious thinking where the subject is approached with great seriousness and without losing the objective.

The supernatural forces begin to interact in these representations where each end has been highly valued, from religious concepts to those of subtle artistic layout.

Eshú, the messenger of Ifá, always present, watches and observes from one of the four faces that are usually destined to him as a faithful guardian of the doors that communicate to two different worlds and mediating between humanity and the divinities, sharing the scenario with different symbols that make and/or affect the consultant. This symbolism shapes the Yoruba cosmology and explains many times the origin and the evolution of things.

Its theme is variable and wide and is related to triumph, devotion, leadership, etc. And so, as like attracts like, these representations are forces embodied to enter into action at the necessary moment. All conform a universe of expression and are ingredients of a great magic formula.

The beings, the things, the objects, and the characters make up the layout of these tables of the future. All interact in spheres and sensitive layers of the thoughts to enter with full vigor and autonomy under the inevitable control of the fortune-teller. The imaginary lines divide the time to be used as temporary expressions by the Awo, who expresses the facts with impressive accuracy.

These lines start from the four cardinal points reflected in the tray where different energies inhabit. They are channeled through the Ashé of the fortune-teller and the mediation of Eshú Elegba or Elegbara as the vital principle for communications.

Thus, the Eshú of the Awo enters into operation as a generating force and a link between the consultant and the fortune-teller, helping to establish contact with the consultant's ancestors who, from the space reserved for them in the "beyond," cooperate protected under the invisibility of their power, and bringing the accumulated experience of past generations.

Within this group can be found the diviners who were part of the religious family and whose spiritual intervention is of great importance and inspiring visionary events. Like mental images, they project into their receiving apparatus, capturing them along with their knowledge to make a perfect diagnosis about the presented situations and fostering clairvoyance and clairaudience and often getting to perceive smells and sounds. All perceptions give a closer approximation to the objective and perfect the prophetic process.

Their names are bearers of power. The more famous they have been in life, the more Ashé they will have at the moment of reflecting the invocations where their presence manifests itself many times as if the forces or the additional energies impel the vitality of those who are invoking them.

This alliance further strengthens the ties invisible to the human eye and strengthens the access of those who are paranormally endowed to access other dimensions. The role of the priest of Ifá is to connect with the forces of nature, listen to them, and know how to interpret them because they want to talk, express themselves, and communicate with beings.

In that regard, the sun, source of life, light and heat, plays an important role. The fortune-teller will try to look toward the East, looking for the benefactor emanations of the star to receive spiritual illumination. He will invoke Eshú-Ogbé, the energetic reorganizer of the primary driving forces of order, to channel the necessary vibrations by giving vitality, strength, and power in the mental projections to the images reflected in the mind that describe situations, so that when interpreting them, he can reveal the future.

The repetition of contact with the superior forces opens the mediumistic channels that increasingly empower the prophetic gifts.

Ifá and Eshú

From the religious point of view, you cannot separate these figures. Hence the importance of mentioning Eshú when we refer to everything that Ifá implies. Both have been connected from the beginning and still are. You cannot reach one without going through the other. They are like two points of the same path that at some point come to touch and merge, having the magical possibility of being in different spiritual planes but synchronizing in one only at a time without getting confused.

Ifá has the mission to trace the paths so that man can walk in search of the secrets of prophecy, and Eshú has the mission to prepare the roads, making them passable. Both work together and the priest cannot separate their sphere of action when he wants to have revelation.

Eshú is restless and unruly unless he is pleased, flattered, and care, for as he deserves. Ifá is orderly and foresighted. Both make up the two sides of the same coin that need to be together to give value to it.

The old legends tell that in the beginning of the planet, both crossed it. Eshú tried to make jokes to destabilize the seriousness and balance of Ifá. Ifá, being always so measured, was bothered by the capacity for irrepressible expansion that animates the spirit of Eshú as his vital characteristic.

One day while walking through different towns, Ifá was circumspect and serious, and Eshú told him:

—*I will cause your misfortune due to my lack of foresight, and my excessive happy spirit will make you miserable. I think the best thing for both of us would be to walk in separate ways. You could walk one path and I on the other. Don't you think so?*

Ifá, upon realizing the situation, answered:

—*If you fall, I will also fall. If you continue living, I will also live. What happens to you, it will also happen to me. This is written in heaven and no one can change it.*

Eshú, rebellious and dissatisfied with the answer, one night left the company of his friend. After stealing a rooster from a nearby village, he cut off the bird's head so he could not tell his partner what happened. Then he kept the other part of the body of the animal in his clothes and returned to his home. When he arrived, he awoke Ifá abruptly and told him:

—*Let's go! Get up! Let's run—death is looking for us!*

Both began to run without Ifá realizing that his friend was dropping drops of blood from the bird to mark the path to his followers. The people of the village of whom Eshú had stolen the rooster were furious and went after the thief's search. The search was easy because of the traces left on purpose as they ran, enraged and armed, ready to retaliate. It was the representation of a pitched scene!

Eshú climbed into the treetop with a single leap. Ifá, transforming into a huge white bird, imitated his actions. Seeing that he was approaching his branch, Eshú told him:

—*Did I tell you that one day I would bring you death and misfortune?*

Ifá replied:

—*If death is for me, it will be for you too.*

The villagers tore the tree to shreds. However, despite the movement and the voices they had perceived, they found absolutely nothing. Where Ifá and Eshú had fallen with the tree, they found a great *Otá* (stone) instead of a thief.

When they raised the Otá to see it better, because they had noticed the intense black color and the shine of the stone, they felt a great heat and a deep headache. They placed the Otá immediately on the ground and said in chorus:

—*Agó Otá, Agó Orí.*

When they looked to the other side where Ifá had fallen, they found a puddle of clear water and received a sense of refreshing relief for their aching and feverish heads. Then they said:

—*Omi Tutu.*

From there on, they worshiped and understood the complex inter-penetration and the parity that united them.

4: Eshú and the Ekedé

Eshú: The Messenger

Eshú is also known by the name of Echú or Exú and has a homologous value in all the representations of the different regions of ancient Africa related to the Yoruba culture. It has the ability to unify the conceptual, immanent, and attractive values of its power.

Eshú is the great messenger, intermediary, and bridge that mediates between men and the Orishás (archetypal configuration of one of the twenty-one paths of Elegguá) and is in perfect contact with the language of the symbols that he uses many times to communicate his messages.

The cause of this action in the world of symbolism is that its irradiation is very close to the most earthly symbolic parameters, acting quickly in imitative magic, where other factors concur to make it faster in its action as being, in its power of observation, always alert presence, restless spirit, vital power and his deep knowledge of the human psyche.

Elegguá or Elegbara was born with the rank of prince of the union of Eshú Añagui and Eshú Alayí Ibere Yeyé. From the beginning of the planet, Eshú Añagui possessed attributes such as the source of knowledge to create wealth and the strength of regeneration appearing in many stories as the mother of Elegguá and in other versions in masculine form as his father.

As the father of Elegguá, he received the honors of commanding and ordering the work and functions of all the other Eshús, as well as the power to designate each one with a different path or name. Of all of them, those that most relate to the functions of a Babalawo, are the ones that we will deepen in their analysis.

The conjunction of elements and factors between Orumilá and Eshú becomes more palpable when we remember that in a path of Elegguá, like Eshú Orungan, he was the faithful collaborator, helpful student of Orumilá. For example, Eshú Ayerú is the one who protects the priest of Ifá, serves him, and collaborates in almost all his functions, becoming a great ally almost indispensable in his task.

Eshú Awo Bará (or Elegguá Awo) is the protector of the house of the fortune-teller, just as he was in the Kingdom of Oyó. Aguado Meyó carries out the same function and is the one who announces the liars, the possible losses or frauds for lies and/or defamations, disrupts gossip and pernicious comments.

Allah Le Ilú is another great Awo of great power and rank, an old watchman and defender of cities, counties, and towns. He is the one who takes care of the territories and the borders of the cities and has spiritual affinity and great respect for the Orno Obatalá.

I also have to mention Eshú Beleque, who is syncretized with the Holy Infant of Atocha. According to legend, Eshú saves Olorun's life (Olofi, as we will see later) and receives a magic key with great power from the Almighty that makes him the owner of the roads. He is considered a clever, insightful, and at the same time very naughty child.

The powerful Eshú Arere is a great fortune-teller considered as the first envoy of Olodumaré to the Earth as his favorite intermediary. He is a great influence through intuition for those who consult the coconuts and is also known by the name of Arere Obí Oké (syncretized with the child held in the arms of Saint Anthony of Padua).

Under this configuration, in many houses of religion with the symbolism of an Eshú-Bara, a specialist is often seen in solving even the most serious labor and economic problems.

They all are ramifications or different paths that, as reflections, obey a single conformation and source: an Elegguá.

How to Take Care of and Treat Eshú

He is the first to receive offerings. He is number one and represents the beginning of things. No request or complaint will be answered without him first interceding.

These were Olofi's orders when he told him that even though he was the smallest, he would act as his messenger, assuring that nothing would be profitable without his intervention to unite earth and heaven.

Once settled, his offering should always be placed near the entrance door for custody or guard to defend the house, the business, the temple, etc., from any misfortune or spiritual attack. It forms part of the four main gladiators of the Santería (the four fighters saints). Next to Ogún, Oshossi, and Osún, he works to disrupt any hint of evil against the protégé.

Eshú-Elegguá, and its various forms of irradiation or paths, governs without interruptions in the open crossroads in the form of a cross (the crossroads, the entrances of the great physical or energetic portals). It also applies to plants, forests, entrances to cemeteries, beaches, etc., presiding and guarding with courage without showing fatigue. Eshú, with his youthful character with which he sometimes jokes, becomes the stereotype of the mocking person when, for example, he takes the path of Eshú Elepó (Eshú of dendé oil) or Eshú Eledú (the owner of coal) who without measuring possible negative consequences, pours oil or corojo butter and coal on Oshalá (hence the prohibition to their children, their Orno Orishás, to consume these materials) when he went to the house of his son Changó, in the kingdom of Oyó.

Elegguá Exú Laroie is well known in the Candomblés and nothing happens to him unnoticed because he knows everything. He knows all the things that have happened, are happening, and will happen in the future. His house is in the terracotta pots along with the other settlements of Exú made of stones or *acutás* and surrounded by iron tools. He likes gold and silver adorned with specific amounts of búzios (cowrie seashells), depending on the path he comes from, and has a crown of seashells on his head (for example, as a messenger from Oxalá.)

It is important to entertain him and take care that he does not miss the offerings of sweets, *aguardiente* (schnapps) with some drops of dendé oil and, of course, tobacco, which is one of his favorite gifts. On Mondays (the day of Elegguá, of Eshú, and of the town of the souls) it is washed with cane liquor very early before the sun is up in the sky, or when it begins to get dark.

This is the way to establish mental or oral communication with Elegguá asking for his protection and work advancement. By cleaning his eyes very well, we tell him:

—*Through your eyes, I should see everything.*

Then we clean his ears saying:

—*That I should hear everything.*

If we follow the necessary steps, all future magical operations will be assured with this type of cleaning.

The remains of corojo butter or dendé, the cigars, and the dust that could have accumulated, or the smoke impregnated with the candles lit in their honor, are cleaned.

The ears and eyes are made up of cowrie seashells (especially the eyes and sometimes the teeth and nose, although this is not very usual and is only done for ornamental purposes).

I have seen these heads molded by hand by experts in these trades and am familiar with the ritualistic liturgy where they represent the shape of the nose with a fairly prominent cowrie. The more prominent, the more olfactory tracking power will be provided to its owner. And everything you track will give you a profit in money (remember the attribute of these seashells as the symbol of the money used by the Yoruba ancestors and as an exchange instrument). I also advise that the owners of Eshú Jelú feed, care for, and clean them with the same method on Fridays since this Eshú is known as a direct employee of Oxalá.

The coconut is one of the favorite dishes of Elegguá and it is also its symbol and representation. Where there is coconut, there is Elegguá. Where it is found, there is wisdom, enlightenment, and protection. As the saying goes, "Where there is coconut, there is wisdom." For this reason it is used in many ebós representing the head, the mind of someone, with different purposes to soften it, reassure him, refresh his memory, etc. One way to revere and entertain him is through light. By offering sweets, your favors will be obtained.

My teachers told me that the coconut represented the World and all the converging points of the Universe and that the coconut was Orí: the head that governed. When the water dried, it had to be refreshed in some way because it was Exú in its seashell or bark and Oxalá in its whitest pulp. The two points and the eternal ends were combined in this fruit because it represented the balance of forces.

The Ekedé

The ekedé is the one in charge of taking care of the vestments, the adornments, and other religious articles in the Candomblés, accompanying also in the mediumistic trance, the Orno Orishá, drying his sweat with a white cloth when he is with his Saint on Earth. Not being a Lao, she is chosen by the priest or priestess of the temple to perform very necessary and important functions, such as those mentioned above.

When the Son of Santo is possessed by his Orishá, he chooses an ekedé approaching the person designated for such purposes. From there, the ekedé chosen by the head(s) of the Terreiro, or by an *ebamí* (a person who has completed at least seven years within the religion), becomes an important part of the cult.

Her main role is to accompany the medium incorporated with his Orishá during the ceremonies, taking care of him in his trance and helping when the time comes for his disincorporation so that everything develops normally. Its importance is relevant and could be considered indispensable. The big difference with the other women who actively participate in the cult is that the ekedé does not incorporate her Orishá.

The ekedés are the great keepers of the Orishás. They are always attentive so that everything works as well as possible. By being aware of all the details in any circumstance, they must be prepared to collaborate and help as much as possible. His task is next to the son of Santo while his incorporation lasts. Despite not being an initiate, her mission is of great value.

When the Orishá begins its dance, it goes toward one of the edekés, grasping her firm and smoothly so that, when subtly placing the hands of its son on the shoulders of the ekedé (that up to that moment was kneeling and with her arms upwards and the palms of her hands as if looking toward the *barracao*, the designated place where public ceremonies are held, as a sign of respect to all the Orishás who had come down to Earth), she understands that she must get up. When selected in this way, she begins her noble helping task.

Dialogue Between Eshú and the Ekedé

An old story tells that one day Eshú met Ekedé. She was very busy and at the same time worried about her duties. Eshú told her:

—*What is going on Ekedé?*

—*I'm tired and exhausted from so much work. I have to accompany my brothers of faith in their mediumistic trances and take care of their clothes of Santo, which is a huge responsibility for me. Excuse me, Eshú, because I'm wasting your time. You also have many things to do, but unlike mine, yours are very important. Again, I apologize for listening to me and lending your valuable attention to me, the least important person in the cult.*

—*Don't talk like that Ekedé. I don't believe it. In a way, you also guide and help men in their communication with the Deities. Therefore I, like everyone else, respect you and love you. I always keep you in mind because you never forget about me.*

—*Then, I want to ask you something that always intrigued me and, of course, I never dared to ask you. Why do you have some misgivings about Oshún's daughters?*

—*It is not revenge, because I do not consider it that way, nor do I feel resentment. It is true that I cannot forget or erase from my memory Oshún's offense. I would like to do it, but I cannot bear that she has used her great beauty to increase my tasks and achieve, through her sweetness, things that others cannot achieve. She really knows how to do spells with her gift.*

—*What do you mean by that? I don't understand, Eshú.*

—*In the beginning, Orumilá granted me the invaluable power of divination. My job was huge because everyone wanted to know what would happen. They did not stop consulting me due to the excessive ambition of men, mixed with his extreme curiosity and anxiety, and that has led them to make many mistakes. You know. Orumilá, who sees everything, immediately understood my situation. By understanding my personality, he granted me the privilege of first receiving any offering and request before any Orishá as a way of repaying me for so many headaches. So that's how everything was granted to Ifá. Things were ordered in such a way that Orumilá began to take charge of divining the future of humanity.*

—*It seems that until then everything was going well, and for that reason, I still cannot understand you Eshú. Please continue if you do not mind remembering it.*

—*Oshún, using her charms and her friendship with Orumilá, began to influence him to obtain the answers that men requested in advance.*

In a way, she was becoming a kind of intermediary. This is the position that, as you well know, only I occupy! Don't forget, Ekedé, that I am the Divine Messenger and the one that transmits the orders of humanity to the Divinities.

—*But Eshú, you say it was only to get the answers to the questions about the past, present, and future.*

—*That's how it was, but when she was not satisfied, she went to Ifá and asked for the divinatory vision. Then Orumilá granted him permission to read the future with five cowrie seashells. My anger is not because she can actually ask the seashells, but it is I, by mandate of Ifá, who should be responsible for the answers. My work, instead of diminishing, was gradually increasing! That's why I understand those who work with care. And you Ekedé, I understand you much better for having committed and self-sacrificed for these tasks. These are the reasons why I clear your ways, leaving you free access to approach so intimately when an Orishá descends on a son or daughter.*

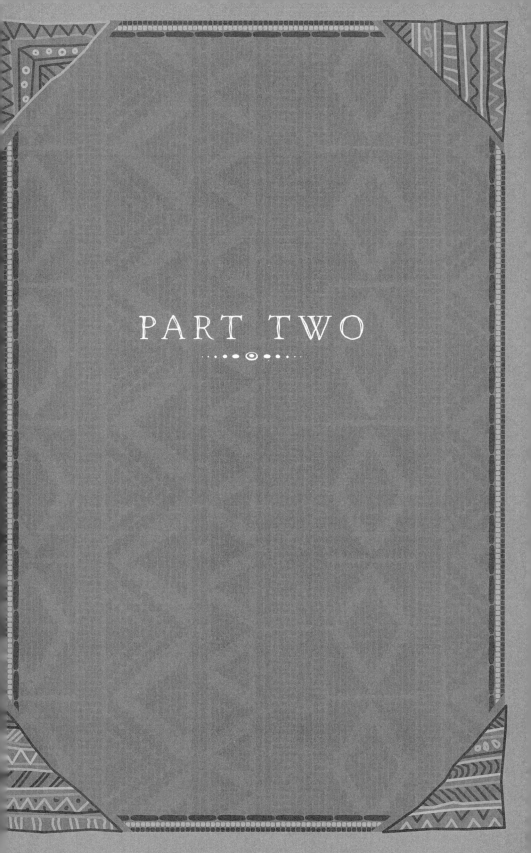

PART TWO

The Art of African Divination

Reading and interpreting with cowrie seashells could be said to be one of the oldest known divination practices, together with the reading of the I Ching, although I consider the seashells the oldest for several elements such as the origin and advent of the Yoruba civilization.

The possibility that the Yoruba people could have been one of the first communities that inhabited the planet, the descendants of the Atlanteans, ancient settlers of Atlantis (a civilization technologically and spiritually advanced that is believed to have existed and died out under the waters of the Atlantic Ocean), is one of the many elements to consider. Many scientific theories argue that the origin of humans began in Africa and that perhaps were dark-skinned. Apart from these two large systems of divination, I don't rule out the possibility of strong connections and influences between them.

But returning to our field of research and analyzing its method of divination and interpretation, one can deduce its high philosophical content and doctrine. Divination is a structured image, not schematized or separate; it is a way of scrutinizing in the past, present, and future with characteristics or symbolisms that could be considered earthly, but with a totally revealing transcendence toward the Great Beyond.

In order to investigate the answers in the purely spiritual realms, the search for a perfect balance between matter and spirit is revealed to us. It establishes between the systems of divination, especially that of consecrated seashells and the intangible world, a perfect communication existing as a nexus to the priest's mind. Thus, the relationship of spirit-mind-brain is conceived harmoniously and wisely.

Each Odú is a written manifestation that, as sacred writing, moves with metaphors ranging from simple dialogues to almost poetic derivations that illustrate the different sobering passages, proclaiming the revealing power of the system of Ifá.

The number four has the power to call into play the four primordial elements of Nature (Fire, Earth, Air and Water), the four seasons of the year, the four cardinal points, etc., establishing a perfect balance with the place destined to read the seashells, or the physical zone where they are to be thrown or interpreted.

Therefore the tray, basket or cloth where the seashells are thrown is mentally divided into four equal parts, and although in practice each roll of seashells is memorized and at the same time interpreted, some soothsayers will prefer to write down their rolls using this type of configuration that is valid.

For this purpose, each Odú can be marked with a single or double line (I, II) vertical and parallel in the second case, interpreting them from top to bottom. Each sector demarcated by the four vertices separates equidistantly from the other four lines that perfectly mark the location of the seashell in the reading.

When the seashell falls open, this position is considered to be masculine and is noted with a small circle (o). When the seashell lands closed, it's considered a female roll and the female side of the seashell or female face, annotating or drawing a cross (+) or an (x). It will be taken into account in which part of the divination territory an open or closed seashell falls in, obtaining a greater interpretation according to the zone of influence (previously determined) of each Orishá.

5: Prayers and Preparation

Obligation of the Priest

Every Son or Daughter of Saint, they who have chosen their guardian angel, their frontal Orishá, also called Orishá of the head, has the right to turn to their spiritual father or mother—Babalorishá or Iyalorishá—in case of any doubt, conflict, or problem of spiritual order, even when these troubles bring with them or entail material factors.

The priest will advise that you take a bath (according to his guardian angel) to dissipate negative influences prior to the reading. He will make an appointment at a convenient time and date for the both of you. In the event that the consult is urgent, he shall arrange and arbitrate the means for it to be carried out immediately, keeping in mind the plan of activities in the House of Saints, the temple or house of religion.

The Son of Saint should greet the room of Eshú. First, he will open the spiritual gates and will grant the consultant the permission to become worthy of the message and response of the Deities. As well as the "Hermes" Yoruba, messenger and emissary, he will intercede before the older Orishás and take their orders, acting as an intermediary and opening their paths.

Then he will greet the Holy Room, and with the priest's permission, he will "beat the head" on the ground (a form of greeting), asking for spiritual elevation and the assistance of his guardian angel. This greeting in front of the home of his Orishá puts him in tune and in intimate relationship with his Saint and at the same time channels his mental request to all other Orishás. The requirements for both the consultant (in this case the Son of the Saint) and for the consult (the priest) are the same: "body cleansing."

This common phrase does not refer to cleanliness or body hygiene (which from here forward is given as a fact) but to the demands required for every ritual within Africanism. These are: abstinence from alcohol, from sex, and in the case of female daughters in addition to those already mentioned, they should not have their menstrual period.

This last concept is really orthodox and conceives the idea that in this state, the woman removes impurities that distance her from sacredness. Not only should you not have previously ingested alcohol, but in addition there should be no carnal desire, or desire related to what is forbidden; otherwise the vibrational field is disturbed and the sacred communication would be impossible between this world and the Yoruba pantheon.

It is no use to have complied with the above but at the time of the consult want to drink alcohol or be sexually aroused. This is equivalent to putting your attention on very material things that aren't predisposed or prepared to communicate with the High Astral.

As for sexual excitement, whether by memories or mental images that are present, it invalidates the sacred character and produces the profane. If you aren't able to keep away from these tendencies, it is better and more convenient to postpone a consultation for another time.

Invocations: Prayers Before Starting to Consult the Seashells

Before starting, many Santeros gather all the seashells in the center of the Ilé Diloggún. It's the place where the seashells are kept, or the sacred area where the seashells will fall. It could be a basket, a white cloth framed by the necklaces, etc.

Many Santeros also place the seashells in a perfect circle, leaving the part open upwards. In this way, they all are prepared to answer by configuring one of the most perfect geometric figures with great magical value: the circle. It is important to try to leave the circle in the epicenter.

In some cases, not only is it intended that the most pointed part of the seashells touch each other, but many Santeros put a coin that has intervened in the spiritual life of the fortune-teller in the middle of the seashells. This is a way of guaranteeing the reward that brings prosperity to the life of the consultant and is a very common practice in some Africanist houses. Symbolically speaking, it is also a material way to link the earthly and the spiritual.

After all the preparations and differentiations, the fortune-teller continues with the pre-established steps in the form of a ritual. Wet the fingers of the right hand in the glass or cup of water and sprinkle the Diloggún seashells three times.

Then, the fortune-teller says:

Omi Tutu, Ana Tutu, Omi Tutu Eshú Elegguá, Ilé Tutu

They continue invoking:

Oddudduá Dadá Orumilá
Babámi Alariki Babá
Olodumaré, Olorun Babá mi
Bake Oshé
Bará Ianá
Kou fie babá mi

Emí Io shiré Babá
Ifá be mi Moyubaré
Orún Moyubaré
Orishálá Moyubaré
Ifá Ago

This form of invocation calls on all the higher forces of good to come together through their energetic influence on Earth.

He also mentions Bara, for the connection of Eshú with Ifá. Then he asks for help from the highest energies, passing through Almighty God and Orishalá, culminating in Ifá, owner of the divination religious services to which he has committed himself.

Then *moyuba* (salute) to the ancestors, asking that nothing bad would happen or occur, and greet the godparents.

The other Santeros are invited to participate by greeting them in this way:

Ashé bogwo igworó, afashé semi lenú.

The fortune-teller takes a small bell, makes it sound by following a circular shape above the Diloggún. This form of greeting is very popular in all countries of Afro-Brazilian influence.

Then, and as a general rule in all currents, one begins to greet each of the Orishás, beginning of course with Eshú, and then with the Saints.

At the end you can say:

Epa ó Babá
Esheé Babá
Agó Oshalá Oromilaia

Here you say:

O pe ó
Yana wa neni
Iré, Iré Awo
Obá Iré
Fun mi ni Ogbon

Fun mi ni Ifá Agó
Maferefum mi
Ashé

There is a request for good fortune and good luck for the fortune-teller and for the head who will direct the divinatory steps and who will become a representative with the characteristic of "royalty" of the voice and the higher energies on Earth. The invocation begins asking for the consent of a type of Oxalá that has to do with the gift of divination: *Oromilaia*.

Force and power are associated in the last word pronounced: Ashé. In all these steps, there may be variations, different invocations, and procedures. The more we know, the richer our vocabulary will be and will increase our field of divination.

Invocations for Each Orishá

Many of the invocations that are used within Africanism have a real power of summoning. Some of them, for example the prayers recited or sung during the ebós (magical works), often tell old and instructive stories. Many have to do with the life of the Orishá that is being invoked. Note the inflection and the different tonal changes in the modulation of the invoker's voice when he implores, asks, exhorts, and cries out with devotion and deep respect.

Like the power seals of the High Ritual White Magic, or like the powerful mantras, all these forms of invocation (whether written on ancient seals, recited or sung) are intended to propitiate, protect, or control an energy level.

Many of those words have a great mystical revealing power that commit a thousand words. Oral transmission has been the basis of the revelation of knowledge within the philosophical-religious history of Africanism in America. This is how I received it from my teachers, from my mentors, and from all those informants who, through so many years of research, helped me collect data of great importance.

And just as in the past we attended the Catholic mass spoken in Latin, and we did it with deep respect even though we did not understand a large percentage of words used in the mass, in the same way the Africanist practitioners who do not fully understand the Yoruba language recite these prayers with immense emotion and mystical anointing because they know that as magical astral keys, the words will open the portals to reach their beloved Orishás.

These are the most used prayers to invoke the Orishás:

Eleggua

Laroie, Eshú Elegguá Laroie akiloye. Agguró tente onú.

Apagurá Akamma sesé. Arele tuse abamula omú batá.

Okólo ofofó, okólo oñiñí, okólo tonikan ofó omoró Ogún.

Oyona alá yiki. Elegguá Laroie akiloye.

Agguró tente Omo. Apagurá, Ashagura Akamma sesé arele tuse.

Abá nundá Ornó babá Ayuba awa Elegguá.

Agó Elegguá.

Ogun

Ogún ñaka nilé Ogún kobú kobú. Alagweré oguó.

Ogún yumusu. Ogún fina malú. Egweleyein andaloró.

Ekum teyú tana guaraguru. Oguñé. Agó Ogún.

Oshossi

Oshossi Odé. Oshossi Odé mata oní bebé.

Orishá Ashé Oshossi. Ede kruesé. Olebure atamasile obeki.

Oké oké aró. Agó Oshossi.

Shango

Eluwekon Ashé Osain. Chereré Adashé. Kokoní jokoki.

Orno lá dufetini. Cherebinú oluoso. Bogwo ayalú koso.

Obá Kosó. Obánishá Kaó Kabiecile. Kaó Kaó Kabiecile.

Agó Shangó.

Iansa

Eparhei Oyá Eparhei lndemuré lndemuré Iyá mi.

Epaieio Epaieio Era Eloyá Sure mi. Oyá Sure awa.

Epaieio Eparhei Iansá. Agó Iansá.

Osain

Osain aké mejí. Oché kuré kere meji bero.

Sakere mejí. Meji le secan, Meji ele seomó.

Eki dibi aguanakero. Osain Ogué-negui Aguado Kuni Kuni.

Ama te le ikú mori. Chase le beriké a yaya. Me-Eú.

Eué ó Ossain. Ué eué. Agó Osain.

Babaluallé

Babaluallé ogoro, nigga, ibba eloni.

Agwa litasa babá sinlao ibba eloni.

Ogoro nigga Xapaná. Ambao Shapaná, Ambao Zapatá, Ambao Chapaná.

Atotó Omulú, Atotó Obaluaié. Agó.

Aggayu Sola

Aggayú Solá Kinibá. Aggayú Larí. Babá—Diná.

Aggayú Solá Kinibá sogún. Ayaroró kini bako.

Egweminiyo. Etalá. Boyubagadaguá. Agó Aggayú.

Ibeyi

Ibeyi oro arabba aíná kaindé. Doin la ó.

Doin Ibeyi. Ibeyi oro alakuá oyé oyé mojojó. Doin Ibeyi.

Beje o ró. Agó

Orishaoko

Orisháoko, ikú afefé. Oro goddó gailotigwaro.

Agó Orisháoko.

Oshumare

Ajun ajun boboi. Oshumaré lo beré lo beré.

Aro boboi.

Aro boboi. Agó.

Oshun

Yeiyé kari. lnba moro ofi kereme.

Ogwa meri kokuasi.

Erí eie ió. Aie iee ió.

Ora ie ieo Oshún. Agó.

Yemayá

Yemayá agguayo o kere okun a limi karabbio Osá ñabbío.

Leggu eyin tebié. Gwa sirueku Yewá.

Obini kuayo, Okuba, Okana kwagna, Keku Yansá Orí eré gwa mío.

Odo Iyá. Odoféiyaba. Agó.

Obatalá

Obatalá, Obataisa, Obatayanu, Obirígwalano.

Katioke okuni ayé. Kofieddenu babá mi.

Ayagguná leyibó jekua.

Babá Oddumila Odduaremu asabbí oloddo.

Babá ayubba. Orishálá aeea ero ola aia aia.

Esheé Babá. Maferefum mi. Agó.

6: Reading with Four Cowrie Shells

Reading with only four seashells brings two types of possible responses that may vary in intensity or have agents or influences that could change the outcome. The feasible modifications start from a set of possible combinations like seeking an alternative or broader response.

The answers would be a yes or a no. Therefore, because the answers are so categorical, a greater commitment is needed in the interpretation and formulation of the questions. The questions must be clear, precise, and leave no room for doubt or misinterpretation.

There must be clarity when asking the questions. There must be objectivity in what we want to know so that in this way the answer is clear, direct, and without distortions or ambiguities. The confusion in the proposal can lead to confusion in the response.

Despite these apparent drawbacks, it is a type of roll used very often, especially because of the speed in obtaining results or answers and also for the simplicity of the procedure. However, even though not only Eshú responds to these rolls, in Brazil they are usually called "jogo dos búzios" for Eshú, or simply "throws with four seashells of Eshú."

Here there is a strong relationship between Ifá and Eshú, the latter as the intermediary in the four roads or cardinal points. Being the greatest interpreter, the servant of the Saints, a path of Elegguá, the messenger between Humankind and the Deities.

When a reading is carried out with four seashells, the priest will not have to mark any ebó (offering) since the answers given by this system only define the different options as yes or no without entering into details or committing to any other answer.

Closed | Open

Different Readings

There are five possible readings or rolls that can be interpreted and/or read. The African names resulting from these five positions are:

1. **Alafia.** Resulting from the four seashells with the open side up.

2. **Eku or Oyeku.** Resulting from the four seashells with their closed side up.q

3. **Ossaran or Okanran.** Resulting from one seashell with its open part up and the other three with their closed part or dented side up.

4. **Meji, Megi, or Ejife.** Resulting from two seashells with its open part up and the other two with their closed or dented side up.

5. **Tau Ar or Etawa.** Resulting from three seashells with open part up and the fourth seashell with its closed or dented part in the same position.

Taking into account the specific forms of these five different positions:

    a. Four seashells have their masculine sides facing **upwards.**

    b. Four seashells have their female sides facing upwards.

    c. One seashell has its masculine side facing upwards and three seashells with masculine sides facing down.

    d. Two seashells have their female sides facing upwards and the other two seashells with their female sides facing **down.**

    e. Three seashells have their masculine sides facing up and the other with its male side **down.**

Even considering them like this, we can do some other correlations or combinations taking different paths in case we're not satisfied with the answers obtained or we have the need to include much more of a developed situation as a response.

In these cases we can combine them and refer to certain rolls within some Odús in order to take into account in a global way what they mean, always considering that they don't represent a direct response to the letter but they're comments that need to be considered.

Meji is the letter that most numbers of combinations gives us, and it could look for points of reference in the roll with twelve open seashells (*Eyila Chebora*), with eleven open seashells (*Ojuani Chobê*), with seven open seashells (*Oddí*), and with four open seashells (*Orosun*).

In this type of combination, remember that when we talk about Ifá, we are talking about the quality of Meji or Melli, whose name accompanies the name of the sixteen letters as we saw above. There is no need to repeat this quality when we refer to the Odús of Ifá because this configuration is understood.

The Five Positions

Alafia

It is a combination often considered to be of passage, or non-defining, and can be taken as ambivalent. When this roll appears, it is necessary to repeat the consult and the answer cannot be considered positive or negative. For many, the most valid phrase would be a "maybe," hence the need to consult once again. Despite mediating this possible misunderstanding of something undefined, it is generally taken as something that promises to be positive and most priests assume that Eshú's response is **yes**. If Alafia comes out again, it means that everything is fine and the roll is reaffirmed because the meaning of the word refers to peace and balance in the karma of the person. It's a symbol of health and good fortune. The consultant will not have any obstacle to achieve the objective. The annotation can be done with four small circles in vertical position.

You can shape a configuration of Eyiogbe in Ifá, representing the balance between orí (head and rational mind) and iporí (the reflection of the consultant in Orún), the perfect combination between the tangible and the invisible world. Therefore it is *emi-pade* (to find yourself), when the consultant has peace, is *Idara*, is well in both beauty of form and substance and represents the state of no confusion, balance, and harmony.

Ifá says that all his steps and decisions bring blessings and good fortune. Your performance is good and acts in accordance with nature. Your karma is clean and in good health. Prosperity will come. Your parallelism with the throw of sixteen seashells brings the Odú *Eyéunle* (eight seashells up) that protects you from any attack. When Alafia comes up and then Meji, the answer is equally positive.

Eku

This roll is totally negative, denoting danger of all kinds and bad omens. It may bring sickness and/or death (Ikú) warnings. When this combination appears, you should throw the seashells again to know what Eshú advises to clean yourself of the influence of Eku and also what the ancestors say, because some ancestor may want to leave a message. In these cases it's best to consult again and ask the *egún*, the spirit of the dead.

When this combination appears, it is recommended to go to Merindiloggún. The questions to Eku will always result in a **no**. For this reason, it is very important to ask a good question so that the answer is accurate and well understood. In Ifá it is endorsed or supported by Oyekún and in the Diloggún by Eyioco. When compared with these two configurations, we will know the origin of the danger and how to counteract it.

Ossaran

This is also a negative reading that alerts the consultant about diseases, afflictions, sorrows, underlying dangers, closed roads, bankruptcies, and so forth. The content is totally unfavorable and may represent extreme hazards or limits. This reading brings a **no** result.

This interpretation is often based on the lack of good things or situations predetermined. With the Chain of Ifá in chapter 8, it is endorsed or supported by Okana, Obara, Iká, and Otrupo. In the Diloggún of chapter 7, is endorsed or supported correlatively by Okana, Obara, Merinlá, and Eyila.

Supported by Okana

The no, or the negativity, comes from appealing to relatives or the people who surround you. You will knock on many doors in search of solutions, but you won't find an answer. The action of seeking or obtaining answers, means, or objects, is compared with the action of travel or walking, as if the person were out hunting in search of food to feed the soul or body. In this case, the figure is associated with Oshossi, the hunter.

However, here the arrow—Oshossi's weapon—will not be well directed and you will not find the perfect target, and there will be the danger of return where you can hurt yourself and be harmed. You must look for other lands and new horizons. Measure your steps and exercise caution, because the animal you are hunting may be crouching.

Supported by Obara

Here, by not acting intelligently and presuming knowledge, you will be allying with the ignorance of those who forget the value of the experience of our elders. The elders have already traveled the road and know the dangers that might appear. You should listen to them and follow their advice. Your pride blinds you because you believe that you own the truth and do not act correctly. Without a change of attitude, results will rarely be favorable and you'll have doubts and insecurities.

Supported by Iká or Merinlá

Dangers come from a process of detriment of the body, and sickness can lead to aging, tiredness, or defeat. Your own words can be destructive and you are advised not to neglect yourself because you could lose your belongings. It is not time to hunt but to defend yourself. The defense also consists in taking care of your body, your integrity, and your health.

Supported by Otrupo or Eyila

Envy, bad thoughts, and other negative behavior involving spiritual and psychic areas are emitted and sent to the consultant. Often their plans and projects will be frustrated by these causes. Ifá advises to be silent and not to talk more than necessary, in particular about private things or of a very important magnitude for the consultant. The less they know about a person, the less they will attract attention and the less jealousy will surround them.

Meji

The path of the consultant is without any obstacle. The consultant is living in truth with valid resolve. There are no problems and the horizon is open. You are protected and supported in your desires by astral forces. Right now your life is balanced, very comforting and special. However, don't be careless, encourage all good things knowing that one way of doing this is by protecting oneself to preserve achievements and peace. Your answer is **yes**.

The positive response of this roll may indicate different origins or paths. To know it, one consults with the Chain of Ifá (chapter 8) and in the Diloggún (chapter 7). In Ifá, it's endorsed by Iroso, Odí, Ojuani, and Otrupo. In the Diloggún, it's endorsed or supported by Iroso, Odí, Ojuani, and Eyila.

Sustained by Iroso

The protection and sponsorship comes from the world of the ancestors, the disembodied beings that care for and watch over the client and instinctively guide him to face their life in different levels and strata. They protect them from any adversity and intuitively present the requirements to be taken into account in case of any problem. Osún, the Orishá who cares for and protects the orí of the Santeros, faithful guardian of the spiritualists, also intervenes and protects them from possible falls and stumbles. From his position, he warns of dangers and inconveniences.

Supported by Odí

The positive response is spiritually endorsed by Yemayá. The element that she presides over (water, the generating power of its seas and the powerful energy of its waves in the breakwater) dissipates obstacles and brings richness of ideas. Because Yemayá is the mother of most Orishás, she brings a message of birth and hope as well as resurgence.

Supported by Ojuani

The yes was answered by the people of souls, and the presence of Oyá is inevitably present, bringing diligence and speed by setting aside any disturbance of unbalanced spirits. Elegguá also intercedes and gives his affirmation by opening paths.

In this combination, the outcome and order are very important. It is imperative not to confuse speed with disorder, neither the viability with the permissible. Throughout time, a solid scale of values will always put you in a pleasant and enduring situation and without only good intentions.

Supported by Otrupo and Eyila

Here the protection and good fortune come from the fire element that revalues the passion and feelings by being endorsed spiritually by Shangó. Your question and concern is fair and valid and speaks of your good spirit exalted by your ideals. There will be action, vitality, and energy in everything that you propose as well as security in what you affirm.

Tau-Ar

News about relatives, friends, partners, and future events is accelerated. It's the revelation about what anguished the consultant. You'll soon know the results discovering the mysterious and all the things that remained hidden or in ignorance. The message refers to the magical and esoteric and can be good or bad. It is advised to take certain precautions to defend yourself. The dynamism of Eshú is in your favor to act with diligence contributing speed in communications.

In spite of everything, you must fight and not lower your defenses to overcome the impediments that may come your way. You should sweep away the impurities that could appear. Your answer is **yes**, but this is achieved with your struggle and tenacity.

In Ifá (chapter 8) it's endorsed and supported by Ogundá, Osá, Ireté, and Otura. In the Diloggún (chapter 7) it's endorsed and supported by Ogundá, Osá, Metanlá, and Merindiloggún.

Supported by Ogundá

The struggle to get yes as an answer is supported by Ogún, the owner and soul of iron. This noble warrior is present to lighten the load and clear your paths of all the inconveniences that you could have. He is anticipating that the struggle will be arduous to get your desires. Nothing will be free and you will get your wishes fulfilled through your personal efforts and having to battle against the enemies who will appear as you develop your plans.

It anticipates that every enterprise will have its battle, but that with its sacrifice and devotion, you will be victorious. You must have the momentum to go to fight for what you desire. You cannot lower your arms during the struggle. Your energy will have to prevail by drawing strength where it is necessary. Ogún will accompany you, encourage you, and help you through difficulties if you work with nobility in your soul. But you must count on your tenacity in all moments, with thrusting force and with the fervent desire to overcome.

Supported by Osá

Here the support comes from the Deity of the winds, Oyá or Iansá who, that with the light of her rays, will provide permanent action and development required in these areas. She suggests the idea of the uncontainable, of what cannot be possessed, what can not be stopped, the speed of the element of nature that presides over us. This influence can lead to uncontrollable variations, different motivations, and different levels of action, often losing the whole vision of the goal.

Oya suddenly arises the swift influence of reflection, making us return to our path. We are stimulated to open the doors of the world of our ancestors, leaving the layer of consciousness that separates us with the Great Beyond, permeable for our loved ones. They're in another plane and from there they can protect us and guide us on our path.

Supported by Ireté and Metanlá

The yes achieved with this combination carries the idea that the consultant should continue with the objective in spite of everything, without being carried away by his lack of optimism. The consultant has a defeatist tendency that he will have to overcome. His negativity could spoil his achievements and hinder his goals. He will have to strive or he could become his worst enemy.

This tendency to distrust your own values and potentials can lead to defeat, and what is worse, the abandonment of pursuits and expectations. You will get what you have proposed or want to achieve only if you reconsider your own vision. Strengthen your ego, reassess yourself, build up your self-esteem. This will be your goal of struggle and effort and thus you will get a resounding yes.

Supported by Otura and Merindiloggún

To obtain your wishes, the message of this interrelationship of the Odús advises recapitulation in the way of facing what has been proposed.

Your struggle to get that yes as a response will have to be directed at the conception and structure of high spiritual levels. You cannot leave aside ethical or moral values. You should revalue the thing or subject in question from an ethical, social, or normative point of view. Karma would play a prevailing role here. Reconsider, listen to the voice of your conscience, and do not neglect your spiritual guides, who will try to get closer to you to inspire you in your tasks.

Combinations with Tau-Ar or Ossaran

From this combination of struggles and sufferings that result in conflicting and unstable situations, innumerable circumstances arise that are good to identify in order to determine the way to approach the objectives.

On the one hand, it is advisable not to allow oneself to be overcome and, on the other, to anticipate suffering in spite of everything. Therefore, it is convenient to ask again and meditate on what we are asking and how to elaborate the question. The question must be clear and objective until a strong response is found. In this way, these combinations can arise:

> **Tau-ar—Tau-ar:** If you roll this in what you want or need, the answer is yes.

> **Tau-ar—Alafia:** You must fight at the beginning. As a result of your insistence, calm and rest will come. The answer is yes.

> **Tau-ar—Eku:** No matter how hard you try, you won't get tranquility or well-being. The answer is no.

> **Tau-ar—Ossaran:** Pain and grief, lack of strength to fight. The answer is no.

> **Tau-ar—Meji:** The reconciliation of forces will achieve a balance. No energetic waste. The answer is yes.

> **Ossaran—Ossaran:** You should not insist. Persistence does not bring good achievements. Misfortunes. The answer is no.

> **Ossaran—Alafia:** Try to bring harmony to your thoughts. Being realistic will achieve the goal. The answer is yes.

Ossaran—Eku: You must totally change your attitude. Turn to the Diloggún and be clear on your questions. Dangerous position. The answer is no.

Ossaran—Meji: Despite a duality, the skies open up and the path is clear of obstacles. The answer is yes.

Ossaran—Tau-ar: There is a high percentage of negativity and confusion, but then the process is reactivated. The answer is doubtful and ambivalent. Please check back.

7: Diloggún: Reading with Sixteen Cowrie Shells

The divination with seashells called Merindiloggún, or in its less known form Erindiloggún, was used by the Omo-Shangó, or "Son of Shangó," the one that has an Orishá as a ruling angel (that is to say it has that Saint established), who naturally had a greater predisposition toward it. They were known as *Yranseé Awo Shangó*. Today, from one end of the Americas to the other, this system of divination reserved only for priests is generally known by the name of Diloggún or Dilogún. Diloggún is abbreviated and originally comes from Erindiloggún, where "oggún" reveals the number twenty, "erin" the number four, and "di" means less. The result of this combination and wordplay gives us the number sixteen.

The *aleyo* (what we call those who are sympathizers, believers, followers, or worshippers of the Orishás but who are not initiated) are forbidden for religious reasons to use acting as manipulators of the game of seashells as a system of divination of this sacred Oracle. This last condition, sacredness, occurs when the seashells "have eaten."

This expression refers to having put them in contact with the Divine through propitiatory rites. Deities speak through these rites, sometimes directly in a particularized way and others together. In spite of this, I would say that it is good and even necessary that the simple initiate or mere sympathizer should approach or investigate these fascinating worlds. Not only would he understand the philosophy and religious doctrine that starts to become sympathy or worship, but he would also be better prepared on both a conscious and a subliminal level to grasp and interpret messages connecting with his inner self. If he had the opportunity and the pleasure to consult with the seashells or with another divinatory system pertaining to the ancient Yoruba religion, he could find himself (*emipaddé*) on the long road that his life has for him to be embodied on this planet.

For neophytes, or for those who have nothing to do with these philosophical-religious currents, cultural training and practice for divination will help them to explore and venture into the entrancing and seductive ways of prophecy using the Diloggún method as learning and recognition of a great technique of divination and, of course, the others that are explained here. All are interconnected with the supreme magic of divination.

The Odús are given different names according to the sources and origins of the different Saint Houses, the Houses of Religion, within many variations. You can find a list of these names in the appendix.

There is often an exchange of names among the Saint Houses, accepted by their use and the custom of each lineage that performs the worship or in the form in which it was learned and transmitted. Many times it is also because many of these nomenclatures fall into disuse, acquiring other words of greater strength or calling power where the priest creates his own code that generally refers to other classifications within this variety.

It must be taken into account that there may be differences and exchanges, all of which are validly transmitted from Father to Son of Saint, or Godfather to Godson. With these sixteen basic combinations or any other group that maintains its unalterable sense of functionality and meaning, we will have to take into account the number of open or closed seashells in each one of them. Therefore, the following positions determine:

One open seashell and fifteen closed seashells.

Two open and fourteen closed seashells.

Three open seashells and thirteen closed seashells.

Four open seashells and twelve closed seashells.

Five open seashells and eleven closed seashells.

Six open seashells and ten closed seashells.

Seven open seashells and nine closed seashells.

Eight open seashells and eight closed seashells.

Nine open seashells and seven closed seashells.

Ten open seashells and six closed seashells.

Eleven open seashells and five closed seashells.

Twelve open and four closed seashells.

Thirteen open seashells and three closed seashells.

Fourteen open seashells and two closed seashells.

Fifteen open seashells and one closed seashell.

Sixteen open seashells.

Observing this numerical determination of the number of open seashells, we realize that it is the rule by order of appearance that is taken for the different related positions previously mentioned.

Orishás Who Speak in Each Odú

A particular Orishá can speak in each of the Odús and is often accompanied by other Orishás who delve into the real value of the letter. All refer to the message they wish to convey in a simple way while remaining rich in moral and spiritual standards.

Here we find that in the different lines of worship, there may be different considerations, and many differ in regards to the Orishá that governs or commands the letter and has autonomy or directional power with respect to the message to be transmitted. Even within the same line there may be differences due to the different religious houses.

Taking into account these considerations, I compiled two lists that I consider to be more current and are part of the Afro-Cuban and Afro-Brazilian traditions. We already know that these two countries were the cradle of Santería in America and that from there it spread to other countries.

In Afro-Brazilian

1. Eshú and Elegguá
2. Ibeyis and Ogúm
3. Ogúm, Xangó
4. Xangó, Yemayá, and Iansá or Oyá
5. Oxum, Yemayá , and Omulú
6. Xangó, Iansá or Oyá, and Oxóssi
7. Exú, Yemayá , and Xangó
8. Oxaiá (Oxaguían)
9. Yemayá , Iansá or Oyá, and Xangó Aganjú
10. Oxalá (Oxalufán), Xangó Agodó, and Oxum
11. Iansá or Oyá, and Exú
12. Xangó, Iansá or Oyá, Osain, and Yemayá
13. Obaluaié or Xapaná and Naná Burukú
14. Oxumaré
15. Obá
16. Orumilá

In Afro-Cuban

1. Echú, Elegguá, Changó, Yewá, Aganyú, and the egunes
2. Ibeyis, Ochosi, Ogún, Orisháoko, Changó, and Obatalá
3. Ogún, Ochosi, Yemayá, Elegguá, Aganyú, and Obatalá
4. Changó, Olokún, Obatalá, and Yemayá
5. Ochún, Naná Burukú, Orulá, and Elegguá
6. Changó, Osain, Orulá, Elegguá, Ochún, and Ochosi
7. Yemayá, Ochún, Ogún, Elegguá, and Obatalá
8. Obatalá, Orulá, Ochún, and all the saints in general
9. Oyá, Obá, Changó, Aganyú, Yewá, Ogún, and Obatalá
10. Obatalá, Ochún, Naná Burukú, Oyá, and Yewá
11. Echú, Babaluallé, Elegguá, Changó, Oyá, Ogún, and Orulá
12. Changó, Osain, Dadá, and Obatalá
13. Babaluallé, Naná Burukú, Elegguá, Ochún, and Obatalá
14. Yewá, Olokún, Naná Burukú, and Obatalá
15. Obatalá, Yemayá, Ochún, Orulá, and Ochosi
16. Orulá

Reading the Sixteen Cowrie Seashells

When the person who is going to consult the seashells is prepared with all the necessary implements, and after having lit a candle for his Guardian Angel, they should have a glass or cup ready with fresh water and have fulfilled all the requirements of spiritual preparation. They deliver to the consultant part of the *ibó*, for example: a small head of a doll, preferably made of wood, saying: *Awonrá Ki Ibó Awonrá.*

The person should firmly hold these objects between each of their hands. The fortune-teller will continue with his prayers and invocations and his orders and priorities may vary.

In many variations of Africanism, it is not a tradition to give these objects. Instead, previously touching the crown and forehead of the person that is going to register with the seashells, he or she is given two seashells called *Addelé*, one in each hand (belonging to a set of eighteen or the set of seashells that form the game called "Seashells of Elegguá," which is made up of 21 pieces).

This establishes a communication between the game pattern, or set of seashells, the spiritual guide of the consultant, and the spiritual guide of the fortune-teller. The ritual lasts for the time it takes the Babalorishá to *moyubar*, or greet the Orishás. Then, the seashells are placed in the basket and the task of reading and interpreting the Odús with the sixteen seashells begins. To prevent the priest from interrupting the consultation with the same question, it is very important that the priest write down in a booklet the name of the consultant, as well as other data and observations that they consider necessary to be used at another time.

Many priests start from the Meji number 13—Metanlá—it is convenient that the consultant goes to see a Babalawo so that he interprets the oracle with greater precision. Others consider that they can advance in the reading and interpret their *erós*—secrets—according to their own preparation, according to the house of religion or their own Ashé that will depend not only on their natural capacity and their spiritual existence but also on their religious family tree.

These are other objects that make up the ibó of the Babalorishá: the efún (type of white clay used like painting to design religious characters), fruits, and other seeds like the obí and the orobó.

The Cuban Santeros, and in general those of Afro-Caribbean influence, add the guacalote seed or a small black Otá stone. The little Otá, together with the efún, are a game of questions and answers that the fortune-teller must put into practice when the letter that appeared brings good results: *Ebboda*. In this case it means that it has Iré, otherwise it would mean *Osobbo*, which is the unfavorable or negative and cancels the good.

When the efún and the pebble are handed out, part of the reading will be defined depending on whether the fortune-teller asks for one or the other hand (the left or the right.) The left hand is requested when the letter obtained is greater or the right one when the letter is smaller. Here is the efún.

The priest asks for the hand that corresponds to the request and, according to the ibó that is there, the answer will be a yes or a no. The efún represents a positive response and the small stone represents a negative. If this is the case, it is an Ebboda position and therefore brings Iré.

Closed | Open

Meanings of the Odús

1. Okana | *One open seashell and fifteen closed*

"The beginning started through the Unity, the driving force of the one, and that's how the World began. From there on, if the good does not exist, there is no evil."

It demands the maximum attention of the consultant because Eshú is preventing him from negative influences around him that bring about arguments, disputes, misunderstandings, and confusions. It may be that the consultant—who lives with Eshú—his friends, relatives, or co-workers are the ones who experience these setbacks.

Be careful with diseases. You must pay attention to health issues and go to the doctor in case of any symptoms.

Your paths are interrupted and your hopes, frustrated. You have economic obstacles and labor problems.

Beware of thefts or loss of values.

Begin with the first step: taking care of yourself. Charity begins at home. If you do not feel healthy, strong, and happy and have a decent job, you'll not be able to help others with fullness and total capacity even if you want to. First solve what is important and what is the priority: yourself. Then you can solve the other things.

This Odú refers to the beginning of the world, where unity was necessary to model the planet, merging into one thing: light and darkness, earth and water, air and fire, night and day, power of contraction and extension, all camouflaged and unified to create a large dense and corporeal mass.

The power of the Earth was encompassing the sky, the water, and the eternal fire from the deep immensities of the center, and from there expanding toward the Cosmos.

From a point of view of Eastern culture, although today it is very common in our Western language, we would say that the eternal balance of opposites was established: Ying and Yang, or masculine and feminine. Both forces were present in the elaborate systematization of the beginnings, looking for the balance to harmonize all things.

Therefore, the consultant must mobilize through this conjunction of harmonies if he wishes to obtain concrete and positive results. The balance must be sought from the inside out as an expression of a healthy and balanced meditation. Only in this situation will they be able to elaborate things, direct them, and project them with firm and not weak bases.

The search for internal balance refers to the existential harmony of the individual with all his past history. You must resolve doubts related to your personal history that covers early stages of your existence. Making these situations clear and trying to cope with them as much as possible by seeking solutions is how the pending processes are revitalized, giving the strength to start and push to begin and concretize your plans.

Patakkí

Just as there is a belief that the Saint comes from the sea as the principle of life and that the seashells are the voices of the Orishás, it is also known that the house of the deities and the connecting bridge of this World with the Sacred Kingdom is the Otá, or the stone consecrated as the home of the Orishá.

If the creation of the stone (Otá) would mark the birth of the Saint, the coconut, fruit, and symbol of Elegguá is what gave birth and strength (Ashé) to the Otá in the beginning.

The legend says that due to the restless and curious spirit of Elegguá (he who sees and discovers everything) he found something round and dark lying on the ground and its shine caught his attention. When he approached and picked up the object, he noticed that it glowed with a strange force but was just a coconut.

The vitality and strange appearance of the fruit did not intimidate him. Instead, it urged him to take the coconut to the palace to show it to his parents. Exactly three days later (Elegguá's number), he became ill and at nightfall his breath began to diminish at the same time that the whitish and reddish shine of the coconut increased. At the end, his life extinguished completely.

The old wise men understood that Elegguá wanted to continue living and that the coconut had received part of his soul. They were amazed, and from that moment they respected the fruit for a long time, honoring and offering gifts because they knew that the soul of their prince dwelt there.

Over time, the older sages died and the legend seemed to lose strength day after day. Nobody remembered Elegguá or the coconut anymore. The saddened fruit stopped shining until it was completely extinguished. Misfortunes such as plagues, storms, droughts, famine, and diseases of all kinds invaded the kingdom of Añagui. The fortune-tellers gathered in alarm, and upon realizing the situation, they sent to check on the coconut, which was rotting behind the door of the palace where the prince had left it.

The Oracles affirmed that they should replace the coconut with something strong, like the spirit of Elegguá, and something hard, like its character and temper. That is how they ordered to place a dark stone in an almost pyramidal shape with three protruding sides that, like the coconut, was white inside and would contain the light of the soul of its owner.

The Otá replaced the coconut and brought prosperity to the kingdom by first receiving the required offerings.

2. Ejioko | *Two open seashells and fourteen closed*

"Rivalry between brothers: an arrow between them."

You are betrayed by people close to you, or by relatives who do not recognize your good intentions by damaging their relationships with negative influences.

Disputes and fights between brothers, or with partners for economic or power issues, will bring moral pain.

In spite of this, if you fight nobly, without lowering your guard and with dignity, victory will be on your side. If all these disturbances brought you financial delays, wait a reasonable time, because later on you will recover your losses with new opportunities to change jobs, places, or workplaces.

If you want the above to take place, follow the advice of this letter and take the necessary spiritual precautions. It is advisable to go back to the beginning. You belong to the natural order of things. Your inner peace is found in simple, natural things. You will harbor a deep love for a family and you will have children; the latter is paramount for you. But remember, the real family is made of people who really love you. Love is a stronger bond than blood.

Symbolically, it would represent a more favorable side to the arrow that crosses the sidereal fields as a messenger of the beyond, and that makes this eternal journey as an accurate message to the Earth to re-value the life cycles. In this way, the arrow strengthens the links between life and death as an eternal passage to eternal life and corroborates the principle of reincarnation.

This could make you think about the person who is your enemy today—you could have affected or seriously hurt her or him in the past or in another stage of life. And the stranger that offers you help right now could be because you helped her or him in the past with some gift or fraternal demonstration.

The example demonstrates the power of the ancestors and how they can return to Earth in different manifestations.

Patakkí

Oshossi walked through the forest carrying his bow and arrows. Tired from the long walk, he lay down under some tree shade. When he woke up, the plants, trees, and leaves seemed to be sheltering him as if to protect his restful sleep. That feeling of peace and tranquility did not make him perceive the figure of the soul and the spirit of the forest that was taking corporeal form between the green mallows and the emerald moss, until it became the figure of the great sorcerer and wise man of the plants. He was the natural herbalist who knew the power of the flowers, fruits, roots, and branches.

Without speaking to him, the sorcerer offered Oshossi his enchanted drink, which is the symbol of the greatest and closest relationship between a hunter and his habitat, the eternal romance between the hunter and the jungle.

Oshossi knew that just as he needed the art of hunting, his bow and the wind that drove his arrow, he also needed to penetrate the forests, plants, mountains, and meadows. He needed to be his ally and his friend to be able to cross them without difficulty. He also knew that only in those places he could and needed to live.

Grabbing the pebble, he said:

—*I accept your drink, Osain, to quench my thirst and renew my strength.*

Osain drank without breathing, without stopping, and without measuring the consequences, even suspecting that the enchantment would make him to fall in love. He accepted the drink despite several warnings from his mother, Yemayá. She had warned him of such an encounter and the risk he could face. She had said:

—*Be careful not to become the hunted hunter.*

From those magical moments, Oshossi never returned to his home. His desperate mother talks to Ogún and asks him to rescue his brother. Ogún walks through the jungles and encounters weeds, plants, and vines that try to trap and stop him. However, just by raising his machete, the plants yield hostility to the magic and power of the Holy Warrior.

When Ogún finds Oshossi, he tells him:

—*Return hunter; return to your home, this is not your place. Your people
and our mother cry out your presence.*

—*No Ogún. I will stay here in the forest forever, in the enchanted forests
of Osain, and if I am charmed by her spells, I do not care. Here, my
weapons are alive and my life as a hunter makes sense.*

Ogún returns on the same path that had led him to this place with
the difference that now he understands the mysteries of the jungle, of
everything that was green and had a life. Now the plants open the paths
in his way until he arrives at the sea.

Yemayá is waiting for good news but soon she understands that the
sea will have to forget about the hunter. Despite having plant life within
its waters, with the same power as those that existed on earth, and also
the large and tempting animals populating her kingdom that could be
captured, Oshossi could not penetrate the waters. He also didn't have
a fishing net because it wasn't his attribute or part of his belongings.

Oshossi understood that his nature represented his union with the
forest. Despite this, his enormous love caused many tears that turned
into white foam that cover the raging crests of waves.

And like Cupid, Oshossi fell in love with the flora without knowing
who had captured whom. However, the hunter cannot be imprisoned
despite how much spell has been drunk, and at some point, or as we
say in different passages and legends, we will see him returning to his
children and wife.

But the truth is that the enchantment of Osain will last forever, and
to be able to hunt its best prey, the hunter will have to go into the forest.

Patakkí

A man wandered through the countryside with no luck. His body
was tired from long walks and lack of food and showed health problems
and low vitality. Without any hope, he went to a nearby town. There he

met a great lieutenant who offered him only a small portion of food in exchange for working in the fields.

Desperate and dejected, he accepted it without calculating the level of greed of his employer. He worked night and day and only stopped to eat and replenish his strength. One day, while he worked the land, an old man appeared in front of him, saying:

—You made fertile these lands, which seemed dead, with your own effort and work, without rest, with seriousness and respect. You must be the son of Orishàoko, the deity of the earth, the protector of the farmers and the crops.

Listen to me. Tonight you will bury in this place, where these oxen are right now, a fruit, a grain, and a vegetable or tuber of each species or variety that the earth has given to you as a sign of its great generosity. In that way, you will see how the earth will make you flourish too and the wealth will come to your hands.

Astonished but with much faith, close to midnight he began to prepare all the things that the elder had recommended. He went to the agreed place and began to dig with all kinds of utensils without realizing that his employer was watching him.

As the days passed, his spirit shone with joy and happiness, and his body became indefatigable and seemed rejuvenated. The landowner, seeing him so happy, began to suspect that what the man had buried so quietly was the product of some theft he had perpetrated against him. The owner thought that was the only reason for this almost incomprehensible situation of satisfaction and real joy, and his greed led him to retaliate.

Unable to bear what was happening, the landowner accused the man of being a thief and, using his influence, ordered to arrest him. After carrying out the corresponding investigations, it was found that the accused had buried only grains and fruits. He had not buried anything of real economic value, or money, or silver, or jewelry, or anything that represented a robbery. As a result, the farmer's fortune grew as did his fame and honesty.

On the other hand, the miserly landowner became even more impoverished when he had to pay the worker with part of his lands for defamation and gossip, as well as for the abuses he had committed in accusing him as a thief. The price he paid for the slander and the false accusations turned out to be very high.

This is how the farmer gained prestige and began to be solicited from faraway places so that his magical hands could recompose the lands to make them fertile and rich.

3. Ogundá | *Three open seashells and thirteen closed*

"Fights, disputes, and discussions: they confuse and bring tragedies."

Hold your position of command and do not let others interfere in your personal things, and even less in matters of work.

Many people will want to take your place, and you will have to defend it. The best thing to do is to reward the righteous and stop the wrong person so that the actions of those who are wrong do not transcend. In this way, you will ensure your position by being active in an authentic and fair process of rewards and gratifications.

In the future, you will smile and rejoice. The nightmares will be left behind and your position will be strengthened and safe without potential adversaries. The throne will be insured for the just and equitable ruler.

Remember, a reign has only one Obá (King) and to exercise its mandate, the sovereign must govern with equality. By taking these measures, what would have been usurped will return, what is lost will be found again, and what is swiped with bad actions will be recovered.

Defend your things and all your belongings, even sentimental ones like your loved ones, for example. Try to avoid fights and arguments because they could be very dangerous. Try not to get exasperated; take care of your nerves. Also, calibrate your actions and measure the consequences and results.

Perhaps your best attack is defense and to safeguard all your belongings. Protect yourself. That is your best way to respond to the real fight; it's a means of survival. The chain of life is based on these uninterrupted movements of struggle, work, effort, perseverance and rest. It's the symbol of the struggle for life. It's essential to rescue these values for your daily life. Discarding them is synonymous with losses and catastrophes.

This Odú, ruled by Ogún, brings you a disposition revalued by courage and bravery. These qualities empower you to battle against all the disadvantages, teach you, and offer you healthy advice not to overcome the difficulties that could arise during the tasks you have undertaken. You can and should fight against difficulties no matter how big they are. Do it and you will see how the horizon begins to clear up, relieving the emotional charges that were stopping your action.

The letter, which means "Ogún creator," manifests and exerts its action in the representation of cutting the weeds and dangerous plants of thorns or poison with the machete. In this way, the paths of men are cleared, letting the light pass to illuminate the good steps toward concrete and fruitful goals. Separating the weeds and harmful plants reflects the true symbolism of the message. It represents the inconveniences and conflicts that are set apart with the strength of will and hard struggle.

Patakkí

The legend tells us about the shame endured by Ogún when, at the beginning of time, he lived with Oshossi, the hunter, and his brother Elegguá.

Ogún, always passionate and impulsive, could not contain or disguise the deep love for his mother. She was always busy and did not realize the internal drama that his son was going through or the huge nightmare that awaited him for not containing his most primitive instincts, not thinking about the consequences, or not being able to distinguish right from wrong.

In his blind impulsiveness, and due to the absence of his father, Obatalá, the brave warrior, had begun to feel physical attraction and desire for his mother. Those desires corrupted his peace and stability and exposed him before the eyes of Elegguá, who was always vigilant and attentive. Nothing was unnoticed by Elegguá, much less the strange behavior of his brother.

Elegguá was confused at first about the situation. The constant gallantries and the excessive care of Ogún, with characteristics that did not frame a true relationship between a son and a mother, made him suspect. Despite the evidence and the fear that something wasn't working well with the altered feelings of his brother, and although they had not manifested otherwise, Elegguá reinforced his vigilance every day.

Without waiting for this to happen, Elegguá did not hesitate to tell his father about his suspicion. The behavior of his brother seemed as if he wanted to fall in love with his own mother. Obatalá, very saddened, decided to come home unexpectedly to see for himself what Elegguá had told him. Upon returning, he heard his wife screaming with desperation. Surprised and fearful, she tried to escape the almost violent insinuations of her confused son.

Obatalá entered the house by surprise, and with a single gesture worthy of a king, he silenced the crude scene and put an end to the situation with his mere presence.

—*Father…*

Ogún said kneeling before him full of shame and discomfort.

—*Forgive me, please. I am not worthy to be your son. I am not worthy of this house, nor to step on the ground that you and my mother step on. I will not have enough life to repent and expiate my sins.*

Don't say anything, I'm begging you. Your silence is my greatest punishment and torment. Suddenly I understood all the evil that I would or could have committed. From now on I will work from sunrise to sunset. I will go far away and maybe time will erase this terrible affront. And as long as the Earth exists, I will work tirelessly. Perhaps that will not make me think of the horrifying and nauseating, the incomprehensible, of my past actions and my unspeakable intentions.

Walking to the depths of the jungle with the help of his machete, Ogún became the great blacksmith, like Ogún Arere, working the metals like a true magician. He insisted on discovering new alloys that could be the constituent elements of swords and other weapons to fight evil.

Despite his noble mission, Ogún had no peace and, deafened by pain, lived the greatest *arayé* (tragedy.) His confusion brought him pain, sorrow, and suffering. Ogún believed that the damage he had caused would never be repaired and that he would never be forgotten and less forgiven.

His mother and his brothers implored before Obatalá. Seeing the desperation of his family and all the good that Ogún had tried to do and his true repentance, Obatalá showed his benevolence and forgave him. Everything was buried as a bad memory, and from that moment on, Ogún became the first soldier under his orders, wielding his sword and spear against the beast and the representation of evil.

4. Iroso | *Four open seashells and twelve closed*

"It's unknown what exists in the depths of the sea."

Your purposes and goals are confusing. You are like an old book where phrases can no longer be read and the webs of doubts and uncertainties cover it making reading impossible. Time seems to have been implacable, destroying its readability and understanding.

Your fears weigh much more than your reality. The darkness of fear infuses immobility, preventing you from planning your life or collaborating with others.

Perhaps your destiny is greater than what you can prevent. In the spiritual aspect, you're advised to follow the priestly path by serving the Orishás and their guides. In the meantime, you will not have a real plan or specific objectives. Do not accept commercial and/or business attempts with ease.

Do not risk money, do not invest wildly, do not lend any property or serve as a guarantee or witness in any event or act. You can lose the material values, your investments, savings, belongings, valuables, or those things that cost you so much to achieve. Beware of intrigues, jealousies, grudges, and untreated or unresolved issues. Beware of those things that seem to have been forgotten but of which that is not really the case.

All of the above may appear because you still cannot clearly specify what is there beyond in the things that are not on the surface or close to your vision.

No one without the prophetic gift can envision things and future events nor prevent everyday actions. Anticipate, elaborate, meditate, consult, and then solve. These are the correct steps to follow.

The decision must be clear. The solutions and answers must be sought with full knowledge and conviction. When a ship sinks, it is necessary to jump into the water even knowing that there is a great depth. In spite of this, the survival instinct arises and gives us the courage to survive.

According to mythology, Osun represents the preservation of the Orí. He must watch and take care of the head, because if it falls, everything falls apart completely. By protecting memory, the values of the past are preserved and the value of experience is brought to the present to plan an accurate future.

This letter highlights the real values in the state of consciousness and balance of thought. The future must be elaborated based on the past experiences transmitted by the ancestors. Hence the importance of preserving the customs rooted in the collective cultural and social memory of the people. It is necessary to honor the ancestors because they are the firmest guide that every society can have to advise new realities and future experiences.

Conducting an *Iba* (a tribute to our dead), we connect with the current world, our world (our inner world), and the ancestral one that brings us wisdom, successful goals, and clear and defined projects.

Patakki

The ancient kingdoms had to grow but their borders were neglected and far away. There were no new warriors or men who could justly rule the annexed territories. Due to this need, the Obá (the king) sent to call all those who were running for future governors of these lands. Talking to them about the need to create sub-reigns that obeyed pre-established norms that had already been proven beneficial and effective, he told them:

—*You must surround yourself with people of your closest confidence, loyal men to the kingdom, and above all, loyal to yourselves. Expert people in each of the subjects and arts should accompany you to make your government a success.*

The mother of Iroso (one of the chosen men) spoke to her son with concern:

—*Be careful, and please do not trust strangers. Choose your companions very well because the distance to these kingdoms is very large, but human greed is usually greater.*

Her son responded:

—*No stranger accompanies me, only my friends whom I know and appreciate without a doubt. I assure you mother: I know their feelings very well. They are worthy and pure.*

The mother of Iroso, still worried, added:

—*Anyway, keep in mind that you are going to distant lands with other seas. Be careful because you could know your friends in depth, but for your own sake and my tranquility, always remember that I know the depth of the sea that is nobler.*

Despite the warnings and pleas from his mother, Iroso went his way without confirming the values of his friends. When they reached a place where they had to go through different caves to continue the journey, the men stopped because they did not know which way to go.

In response to the situation, Iroso took the initiative and decided to be the first one to enter a cave that gave him more confidence because, from the outside, the others seemed dark and impenetrable. After entering, his friends grouped themselves like birds of prey and planned how to take the reins of the expedition. They decided to remove from the command, the one that until that moment, they called their ally, their leader, and their "friend."

The plan consisted of killing him to usurp the titles that accredited him as future regent of the new lands. They hid and advanced until they almost reached the other side of the cave where it was a little brighter. Iroso was concerned about the delay of the group and began to worry when he remembered the warnings and advices of his mother. Without knowing why, he began to prepare to defend himself against something or someone without knowing for sure the reasons. Through screams and wielding their weapons, his treacherous friends wanted to intimidate and kill him.

Iroso did not have the need to defend himself too much. When he was ready to fight against the traitors, he heard the words of his mother as if she had been next to him saying:

—*... but for your own sake and my tranquility, always remember that
I know the depth of the sea that is nobler.*

In that instant, big waves suddenly entered the cave, disrupting the plans of their enemies, throwing them far away and stunning them in just seconds. Yemayá had made herself present with her great mysteries. Like every mother, she had taken pity on Iroso's mother and listened to her prayers asking for her son's protection.

5. Oché | *Five open seashells and eleven closed*

"Blood is life; they both run through arteries and veins. Blood and life are one thing. For this function to take place, your heart pumps, and the uninterrupted flow of life does not end."

This Odú refers to a very sensitive and emotional person whose hypersensitivity can lead to behavioral problems and physical disturbances. In these cases, it is advisable to consult an expert who is experienced in these matters.

You experience continuous setbacks that make you lose all the things you love, longed for, and appreciated. These losses are intimately linked to your karma and represent the different tests you must confront. Oshún is warning you about what is most advisable for you. She refers to the convenience of entering the path of spirituality. If you inquired and asked questions demonstrating interest in the metaphysical and spiritual, it is convenient that you deepen in these fields.

If your beliefs allow it, it would be ideal for you to solidify your Saint, to enter into the Law of Saint, in the Rule of Ochá or Oshá (Santería), or that you connect to any of the Africanism currents because your soul carries baggage and the accumulation of experiences in this regard. Your Orishá will bring you spiritual peace and your problems will be solved. This is the time to do it. Perhaps before it was not the right time, and even if you can do it later, it is convenient that you do it as soon as possible.

This action could compromise your karma by hindering your path and delaying your things. However, you are the one who decides the time by evaluating your spiritual, physical, and/or material needs.

Any philosophical or religious current that you decide to enter that has as objectives the truth, justice, that is based on good actions under a concept of entity, and has the sole purpose of achieving spiritual perfection will be satisfactory. This will help you to evolve as a human being elevating your soul and refine your most advanced feelings.

Remember, this letter clarifies that your Guardian Angel, your Orishá, is the one who is choosing you and offering this opportunity. This Odú also tells you that Oshún brings joy to your life. She will wipe away your tears and if you still have no partner, she will put the beloved on your path.

You will change your life and perhaps your home, establishing a better and new future without discouraging clouds, depression, and melancholy. In this way, you will recover from any adversity. Remember, the most important thing for you is to love and be loved. Fight to always achieve it. This is your reason for living.

Oché is the symbol of beauty, prosperity, and abundance. Use the value of the letter as a clear and quick enchantment to achieve these things and be able to recover from melancholy and failures.

Oshún keeps and treasures all these secrets. Not in vain, she is the great magician with knowledge of great ebós. If you follow the right path, her spiritual advice, good fortune, and prosperity will grow with her refined and gentle magic.

Patakkí

The history of this Odú refers to the two errors most disapproved by humanity: vanity and betrayal.

Let's see what the legend tells us.

One day, Olofin gathered all the birds to compete for their beauty, personality, charisma, and personal attributes. All the birds began to practice their flight immediately. Some stayed floating for hours in the air as if playing with it. From dawn on, they stood at the tops of the trees to rehearse their songs, and between whistles and songs they began the day bringing joy and hope.

There was a parrot that did not stop mocking all the birds and boasted its delicate feathers, the bright color of its plumage, and above all, its ability to imitate the human voice. The parrot argued and told the other birds that he would win the competition because there was no other bird that could imitate and repeat the voices of all humans with extraordinary accuracy.

The parrot was talking too much and not stopping. Not only was he annoying with his repeated speech but many of the birds began to feel jealous and envious and the strong desire that such a boastful animal had nothing more to boast about and wished him the loss of his attributes.

Thus was born the mother of almost all other sins. What at first was a symbol of joy and brotherly unity among the birds, ended up being an unfair and corrosive contest. Many of the birds, whom had let themselves be dragged by these low feelings, flew to very high peaks. At the top of the mountain lived an old man who, away from everyone, practiced black magic.

The hatred that the old man felt had turned him into a malignant and resentful being and had separated from his loved ones and people in general. The birds flew to the place where the sorcerer lived. The winds blew harder and harder and the effort to get there was greater. Tired and exhausted, the birds arrived at the precarious house of the old man. After listening to the stories, the sorcerer gave the birds *Ofochés* (haunted powders to cause damage) and recommended that they be thrown at the parrot's wings and head as closely as possible. That would cause the parrot total instability.

When the day of the contest arrived, and just at the moment when the parrot passed in front of the jury, a flock of birds flew very close, almost touching it, and dropped the malignant rain of the enchanted powders. The parrot began to rave. His talkative tongue did not stop saying incoherencies. Their feathers became opaque, losing all shine. The instability that the parrot was suffering made him fall and roll to the ground. It was a sad and lamentable spectacle.

Suddenly, the voice of Olofi was heard saying:

—*There is no greater beauty than the soul or greater recognition for the soul that vibrates more and more in harmony and fullness. Far away are those who are puffed up by their attributes and are also far away who envy what does not belong to them.*

Everyone will get the reward they deserve. Those who stayed out of this sad episode will tirelessly fly from land to land, through the continents, so high that no soul can match them because the greatest beauty is the priceless gift of flying.

And as a lesson from now on, the feathers of the parrot will become the most effective weapon to counteract malignant dust.

For the others, the intriguers who have already flown very low, they have managed through their evil plans to be closer to the dark than to the light. For them I say these words: they will never reach the height in their flights, nor the speed they once had, until they are again worthy of it.

And he ended by saying this sentence:

—*May the sadness that today overwhelms us all serve as a lesson and never corrupt the fraternity among all. So be it. Ashé.*

6. Obara | *Six open seashells and ten closed*

"A true monarch does not rule with lies."

Chimeras and illusions are only unrealistic fantasies. Discard them, do not consider them or allow them to transmit unreal ideas or thoughts.

Be coherent and concrete. Do not lean toward a modality that supports or allows you to slip away from reality using lies or omissions. Speak the truth without allowing anything to be twisted.

Dreaming is not bad, but always living in a world of illusions is regrettable. The exaggeration increases and distorts the concepts of reality.

If you deal with justice, do not judge in vain or issue unreliable statements. Manage yourself with prudence and truth.

To govern your life, in the full extent of the word, is to do it with justice and truth in deeds and words. Otherwise, you cannot be your own leader or know where the real or the false begins.

This letter recommends coherence and balance in the procedure, putting the truth above all in a realistic and practical sense. If you cannot achieve it exactly, do not make judgments or opinions that could seriously compromise you on issues of real value.

The greatest fantasy and incoherence can be greed and excessive ambition.

The letter advises a balance between earthly desires and spiritual values.

It is essential to measure what is just and necessary to accurately calibrate your opinions, your judgments, or the steps that follow.

It is advisable not to get carried away by hasty opinions not faithfully verified in a reliable way.

False or erroneous parameters, as well as unreliable reference sources, are really dangerous. Remove them and discard them from your path.

Meditation and depth of thought are advised in search of a deep analysis of situations.

Every ruler fulfills their functions with a single purpose, with a single goal and a single objective that is to govern for and on behalf of the people.

Your interests should not be other than those of your community and your society. You have to set aside or discard personal ones. You must remember that coherence and truth must prevail in your actions.

The prosperity that you could achieve should be maintained with humility and without boasting or strutting. It is advisable to keep silent when envy occurs. In silence you will discard jealousy and negativities. Keep silent and you will prosper.

Disclose what you have and unfortunately you will lose everything.

Stealth is also recommended. Prudence and secrecy are your best allies for your true success.

Prudence when you speak and reserve in your manifestations, along with a generous soul, are the ingredients for absolute and total triumph.

Patakkí

A great party was organized in the palace of Orumilá, and the Orishás prepared all their gifts with great excitement and enthusiasm. The preparations had to be very careful for such an important event of great magnitude and no detail should be left aside or left to chance.

One of the Orishás, however, was very worried and had his sight lost in the horizon as he was looking for a way out. The Orishá seemed to observe something unattainable as infinity in the solutions he wanted to find.

Through a deep meditation, Osain wanted to perpetuate the moments that temporarily distanced him from his real problem and so he wanted to solve his grief. Shangó came to his door and, surprised to see him in that situation, said:

—*Osain, kilo se? (Osain, what's going on with you?)*

Osain responded with a melancholy look and a gesture of deep depression. Shangó interrogated him with energy asking him about his attitude and said:

—*Osain,* ki le yi! *(Osain, what's that!)*

The great herbalist walked uneasily until he said:

—*I am very ashamed. I feel so bad because I, just me, do not have enough fruits to take to the big party and important occasion. I only have* inhames *and* abóboras *[pumpkins]. My harvest was very poor this year! I, the owner of all the leaves, the plants, and their fruits, feel humiliated and inferior to the other Orishás. I feel sad because* aiyé nilé mi *[the land in my house] is not* Iowó *[rich this year], and therefore, I am not either.*

And he continued telling Shangó:

—*You can imagine that in these conditions I will not be able to attend and greet affectionately.*

When brought to him, Orumilá asked Shangó:

—*What are these* abóboras *that you have set aside and accommodated so carefully, highlighting their presence and differentiating them from all other gifts?*

Shangó answered with great dignity as he recounted everything that happened.

Orumilá took a single abóbora, squeezed it between his hands, and blew it six times. Then he placed it above the others to which he also blew but more slowly. Looking back to Shangó, he said solemnly:

—*Take these fruits, already blown, back to Osain.*

Shangó departed back and explained to the great herbalist everything that happened.

Osain was confused and sad. A few days later, the hunger increased among his family, and his wife asked him desperately:

—*Please Osain, cut one of those fruits that Orumilá did not want.*

Osain agreed and began to open one by one with the help of a blade.

His surprise was such when he discovered that inside the first fruit, and then in the second, and in all the rest, there was money. The reward for his humility and dedication had come as justice to favor and reward the lack of greed and arrogance. Now Osain was rich, powerfully rich!

Patakkí

Obará was part of a family of sixteen brothers called in the same way as the sixteen Odús. His family was always distanced because of his poverty and the humble conditions in which he lived.

The other fifteen brothers were wealthy, powerful men, business people, and wealthy merchants who despised their brother for not having the same economic equality. Every year they consulted an Ifá priest to find out how they could preserve or increase their wealth even more.

In one of the consultations with Ifá before the end of the year, the fifteen brothers asked the Babalawo how to maintain their wealth. The priest predicted:

—*Riches come altogether, however, you do not seem completely united. Are all the brothers together? Or is someone missing here?*

They answered in unison:

—*Yes, our brother Obará is missing, but he is poor and we are not interested at all.*

—*In the most insignificant or poor is sometimes the true greatness of wealth.*

All of them looked at each other and took the Babalawo's response as a metaphorical and moralistic phrase.

When they finished the consultation, he told them:

—*As usual, I will give each of you a present. I want to be generous and at the same time equitable, and the only thing I have in quantity of fifteen are these abóboras. Take them and be happy.*

The fifteen brothers left disappointed by the humility of the gifts, even knowing that after consulting with a priest in Africa, he symbolically delivers some present to his consultants. The brothers talked and made fun of the situation and were offended by so little a gift.

One of them finally exclaimed:

—*Let's all go to the house of Obará. There we'll eat and we'll spend the night, and the next day, we'll return to our homes. But first, we will leave him these insignificant gifts.*

Obará and his family received the brothers with open arms, and due to his lack of malice, he did not ask questions. The brothers ate almost treacherously everything that he could offer, and the next day they left not without first giving him the fifteen abóboras.

For almost six days, a windstorm lashed the place without stopping, and the little reserve of food they had left was running out. Obará told his family:

—*Unfortunately we will have to eat what my brothers brought as a gift.*

When he opened the first of the abóboras, he found a large quantity of gold coins that came out of the interior without ending. It happened with the rest of the fruits. Huge riches sprang up: pearls, precious stones, gold, silver, and other incalculable metals.

Surprised by such a fortune, Obará was perplexed and almost paralyzed. Then he heard:

—*Don't tell anyone. Do not say anything. Keep the secret to save your wealth.*

That voice advised discretion and reserve.

As the months passed, his wealth increased and that of their brothers decreased. His worried brothers decided to go back and consult another Babalawo who told them:

—*Riches come altogether, however, you do not seem completely united. Are all the brothers together? Or is someone missing here?*

—*Our brother Obará, is missing, said one of them.*

Another brother added:

—*Now he is the most affluent of all of us.*

The fortune-teller continued:

—*All of you, when you rejected the humble things, you rejected the wealth. Inside what you gave to your brother was true fortune. That's what turned your brother into someone wealthy and powerful. I'll give each of you a coin and you'll keep it for the rest of the year. However, I cannot predict much prosperity for the rest of the year. Yes, in the abóboras was and is the key to everything.*

After listening to the final words of the fortune-teller, the desperate brothers ran to the house of Obará, struggling each other to arrive first so they could claim what they considered was still theirs. When they arrived at the house of Obará, they found that the house was not the same as before. Now, in front of them, there was a real palace.

—*Give each one of us the abóbores we left in your house!*

They shouted repeatedly in a somewhat violent way.

When Obará was going to answer them, he heard the same advisory voice that had alerted him repeating the same message:

—*Don't tell anyone. Do not say anything. Keep the secret to save your wealth.*

Obará responded immediately, pointing to the ground:

—*My brothers, here is what you're asking me; some of the fruits are already rotten and others were eaten by the pigs.*

Disenchantment and disappointment were framed in the faces of his ambitious brothers. The oracle had not been wrong. Behind humility, there was great wealth.

7. Odí | *Seven open seashells and nine closed*

"At the beginning there was a huge hole. Then, where the hole was, it filled with water."

"At the beginning" refers to the beginning of time when, according to philosophical concepts, it's believed that chaos existed before order. Taking into account the state of preliminary confusion, the balance was then established.

The metaphorical meaning of the image of a hole refers to a great capacity for conception in the future. The hole fills with water, creating a visual duality, since it can hold and retain water. It can also have the capacity to make everything fall into an eternal hollow without horizons or ends. This duality means that when this letter is presented with Iré, it brings something beneficial by doing ebó and obeying what he asks for on the way.

On the other hand, many consider it as the worst of the Odú because it presents all the possible misfortunes. The consultant should take care of diseases that can be epidemic, eruptive or infectious in nature. It is recommended to protect your partner and your home without allowing any kind of disloyalty by anyone.

Your energies are disassociated and there are disturbances in the seventh chakra that produce nervous disturbances, sleep problems, and insomnia, allowing spiritual attacks while resting. As a result, you suffer from lack of energy and loss of vitality during the day. The first and second chakras are also affected by harmful influences and may be attracted to performing harmful physical, moral, or spiritual practices such as drug addiction or alcoholism.

It reflects a person with sighted ability and signs of hypersensitivity. This approach is recommended to have one more weapon to defend oneself on the psychic levels and take care of a possible fragility in the character and mental structure.

The extreme meaning of this letter refers to the word "Odí" and its symbolic representation in the configuration (enough), which is finished or sealed. By revealing its character, it closes the gap according to the metaphor, reinforcing through ebós the advice of the Odú and assuring the non-concretion of the described misfortunes.

The word *To* in the Yoruba language means "the end" or "the top" of something. It represents the limit of Odí as a metaphysical symbol, not as extermination, but the continuation of something transformed.

Patakkí

Here it manifests itself by the force of Eshú, opening the energetic channels to give birth to the beginning of all things through the use of such a magical and revealing number: seven.

Eshú is the symbolic representation of the disorder prior to equilibrium, and in its actions bring the beginning of good times and prosperity. From the immensity of the subconscious emerges the mythical figure of Eshú creating great depths to give greater capacity to the water that would cover most of the planet later on.

Other stories attribute these geographical depressions to Eshú. The mission is configured as the first one issued by the Almighty that sends to the Earth innumerable forces considered primary in the energy echelons. Its function seems to be to create the first furrows for the psychic life that would have to nourish the base of life: water.

Eshú, the divine messenger, delivered this epic to the canalizing and liberating water of phallic energy so that it would spread everywhere and collaborate with fertilization and mineral enrichment. His magical presence was considered fundamental. As a result, every living being from the depth of the earth could enter into action as a nervous network to promote future changes. Eshú, the owner of the roads, walked on the surface and left behind signs that only time and the action of climatic agents were modifying.

The water ran through and covered the furrows and its wake was appeasing the vehemence, the rage full of ecstasy, and the euphoria of *Hermes Yoruba* to then temporize and harmonize with all forms of life on the planet. The messenger opened the roads to the mother of the Orishás, Yemayá, so that she could extend her maternal gifts. From her breasts or from her womb (there are several stories that differ), life sprung and the waters covered everything. This was the first indication that enabled the permanent capacity of fertilization.

Yemayá, kind as any mother, is also incomparable in her just reprimands where she teaches her children lessons of humility, honesty, and benevolence. In this way, Yemayá, with seven roads or avatars, populated the entire Earth and made it eternally fertile and prosperous, representing the complex and balanced mechanism of nature.

8. Ejéunle | *Eight open seashells and eight closed*
"The head directs the body, there is only one monarch for the people and only one head in a body."

You are a person with a great capacity to love, with high fraternal feelings, and with gifts of charity. From a young age, you will stand out for having a very concentrated, almost shy personality, often preferring intellectual activities to physical ones. It is advisable not to ignore them because by putting them into practice, you could help relieve the stress caused by things, like emotional burdens that you do not know or cannot divert to avoid being hurt.

With a great interior capacity and with the experience that taught you to treasure, you are prepared to rule and govern. You refuse to be directed and only accept it when the direction comes from someone you consider superior. Your admiration for that person allows you to receive advice, guidance, and often indications or orders.

However, you must learn to earn the respect of others and not allow yourself to be underestimated. Those who know your altruistic ability could take advantage of this situation and could try to cheat and/or hurt you.

You will be attracted to the spiritual, thanks to your special sensitivity. Many times you are associated with the artistic. Your expressive gifts, abound and varied, and you should encourage them by specializing in those that feel closest to your soul. You have the spiritual ability that leads you in that direction. You should be a saint and be part of a religion.

Although you will always be criticized and envied, these negative thoughts will not affect you and, on the contrary, will strengthen your character. Your personality will be molded and shaped like a great leader. You will have the skills to train, prepare, and teach disciples and create your "own school" thanks to your style. You will awaken in a world full of psychic sensations since this letter represents the light of knowledge and wisdom.

You will undertake the wonderful path of being able to connect with the higher Astral planes. You will be the mystical reflection of those who seek the truth as a form of response, as well as the motivation that will encourage you in difficult moments to give you serenity in your spirit.

You must keep ethical-moral values very high to preserve the power that will increase over the years. If you achieve balance within yourself, you will enhance your spirit that will benefit your life.

But if you are foolish, the power will seem to disappear, your hands will be annulled and you will have lost the greatest treasure: the humility of the powerful.

Patakkí

The king and his daughter lived in a great palace. They spent a lot of time together and took care of each other. However, the king was very jealous of the princess and would not let anyone approach the palace. They lived far from their town and he only cared about collecting taxes.

The ambition and selfishness of the king prevailed above all. Despite the advice he received on how to take care of his daughter, she had begun to get sick from an inexplicable ailment, he ignored anything that was not of his own interests. He did not let the princess be exposed to the healthy rays of the sun. She paled day after day and was weakened and depressed due to the lack of natural light.

The poor daughter, already almost prostrate and without strength, insisted to the king to let her lean out of a window and breathe fresh air for at least a few seconds, but her blind father refused. One day the energies of the sad princess diminished.

The desperate king went to Orunlá, asking him to visit his daughter in the palace. Orunlá was very busy and responded that it would be impossible due to his occupations that coincidentally were also related to health issues (among many other things) of many people who had been waiting for him for a long time to define their ills, channel their cures, and take care of other necessities.

Instead of going to the palace, Orunlá insisted that they appear before his presence and invited the king and his daughter politely to visit him. He also clarified to the king that in this way the custom of not allowing anyone to enter such a fortress would not be interrupted and would remain intact to maintain the king's tranquility.

The king, offended in his dignity of monarch, was obfuscated at such impertinence, because in his mind, there was no greater king than himself and there were no higher priorities than his. But because the young princess's health was getting worse, the king accepted the invitation with resignation.

The king and his daughter arrived on the eighth day at the house of Orunlá. Without realizing that the doors were lower than his height, the king hit his head hard with the door frame. The blow caused his precious crown to roll down the steps. The king was desperate in the attempt to recover the crown and forgot the real reason for his visit. He did not notice that his head was bleeding from the blow received.

Orunlá said:

—*You have hit your head awkwardly. Your guardian angel feels offended and obfuscated with you for your vanity and pride, and as you see, the symbol of your power is on the floor.*

The people, saddened by the illness of the king's daughter, waited impatiently for the news. When they saw the monarch's crown rolling down the streets, the people understood that the causes of the princess's illness were also rolling downhill because they had to do with the arrogance and excessive pride of her father. The crown, symbol of the king's absolutism, was in the middle of a great puddle of mud. People ran to pick up the crown to clean it but they realized that it was dirty even before it got muddy and that it was better to hide it so that the sovereign's wrong behavior would never make his beautiful daughter sick.

Orunlá ordered the monarch to make ebó. He told the king that in order to recover the princess's health and to clean his crown and head, he should gather a piece of all white things, then place them inside a white cloth sack and sprinkle powdered white egg on top while asking Obatalá for the peace of his people and the welfare of his Orí.

—*If you do so, your daughter's health will improve, she will lose her pallor and her excessive whiteness will disappear, and the white will be in the king's soul. That's where it should be.*

Orunlá concluded with total firmness and sweetness.

9. Osá | *Nine open seashells and seven closed*

"Your best friend is also your worst enemy."

This letter is stormy and reveals that the client goes through difficult and decisive moments at the same time. They are compulsive thoughts with irrepressible desires wanting to take immediately and untimely all the things that cross their path.

In the face of such despair, your movements are quick but not careful and without thinking. Your outbursts can lead you to carry out disastrous actions that you may regret later and will be very difficult to repair.

Problems appear with your partner, such as arguments and confrontations that often start without knowing the causes that motivated them.

Outside agents are working against you so that you cannot coexist with your partner, or with your parents, if you are single and still live with them. The purpose of these negative forces is to destroy and annihilate any sentimental or loving relationship.

Calm down, take it easy and you will control the situation. Everything must be done in a comprehensive and contemplative manner, discarding the desires from fighting and arguing. Follow the ebó that marks this Odú and everything will be just fine.

Make offerings to Iansá egún nitá, the owner of twenty-one egunes. She will appreciate your actions and will protect you. Also, try as much as possible not to visit cemeteries or attend wakes, don't visit people with serious health issues for at least three months.

Invoke Ogún to defend you and Obatalá to bring peace to your mind and happiness to your spirit. You must request with prayers and prayers to Yemayá for the durability of your marriage. She will listen to you and take care of your partner or marriage. The letter advises to move away from the untimely and instead seek calmness and patience by discarding outbursts and the desire to modify or alter all things without previous analysis.

This Odú represents the hurricane force of the winds in the configuration of Oyá or Iansá.

In antiquity, when this Odú came out to mark the future of the regions and the towns, it often referred to the elemental forces of the air that, in an unbalance of the collective Karma, could strike the Earth for having been offended and transgressed the universal natural order.

When it is on a personal level and does not bring Iré, it can trigger stormy passions at all levels with serious consequences, sentimentally carrying loneliness, jealousy, estrangement, separation, or divorce.

From the physical point of view, it is related to fatigue, illness, psychophysical disorders, apathy, loss of freedom, physical detention, etc. From the spiritual point of view, it refers to the lack of peace and harmony. And from the economic point of view, it refers to the monetary damages such as the loss of work, unemployment, bankruptcies, thefts, bad investments, and excessive expenses.

Patakkí

History tells us that Obatalá (or Oxalá) had left his lands to go in search of his wife, Naná. After previously consulting Ifá about his trip, he had been advised not to travel because he could have great difficulties. It's not the right time to look for his wife. Obatalá, determined to find Naná, and emotionally disturbed, does not pay much attention to Ifá and leaves for the kingdom of Oyó.

The only strategic measure he adopted to avoid suspicion of his rank, was to leave his clothes and emblems of king and dress in common clothes of the people. Shortly after starting his walk, he meets Eshú Eledú (the owner of the coal) who, disguised as a poor old man, tells him:

> —*How lucky to find you on my way, pilgrim! I feel very tired and fatigued and I cannot bear to carry this bag anymore. Neither my arms nor my shoulders can carry more weight. Could you please help me to carry the bag for a while?*

Obatalá accepted and lifted the heavy load by placing it on his shoulders. Suddenly the bag opened and all its contents fell on his clothes. Coal fouled his clean clothes. The King of the Igbós put aside his anger and for the first time remembered the words of Ifá. He quickly went to a stream that was nearby to wash his clothes and continued his journey.

Supported by his staff, Obatalá meditatively walked slowly toward his son's lands. Suddenly, a man appeared screaming in pain and complaining about the excessive weight of the decanter he was carrying. Letting himself be carried away by his good feelings, Obatalá took the carafe of the hurting traveler, and without realizing that it was uncovered, all the liquid in the bottle began to spill over him.

Laughter and mockery sprang from the owner of the carafe, who was none other than Eshú Elepó (the owner of the palm wine). Once again, Eshú became a great ridiculer, laughing at Obatalá, staining him with dendé oil or corojo butter. When Obatalá tried to take off his stained clothes, Eshú had already disappeared.

Very sad and mad at himself for not having paid attention to the recommendations of Ifá, Obatalá returns to the nearest river to wash his new clothes. Without resting a single minute, and in spite of all the inconveniences, he heads off into the dark night with the sole objective of reaching the kingdom of Oyó as soon as possible.

At dawn and in the middle of the forest, Obatalá can see in the distance a beautiful white horse that grazed in the meadows. When he observes his whiteness, he realizes that it is the horse that in the past he had given to his son as a pet.

In this part of the story, some priests claim that the horse had been stolen from Shangó. The King of Oyó, desperate for the loss of his beloved animal, orders to seek the thieves. His guards meet an old man in ordinary clothes riding the horse of his Obá. The old man, confused and perplexed by the irruption, cannot prove his innocence or explain that he had been tempted by an unknown man to ride the animal. The old man, unable to prove his innocence, is taken prisoner. (In this other version, Eshú would be the unknown man who offers the horse to Obatalá.) From there, the children of Obatalá are forbidden to use dendé oil or ride horses and have something to do with the soot.

Continuing with the previous story, Obatalá runs with happiness when he recognizes the animal, takes it from his mane and tries to take it to the lands of Shangó. Obatalá is surprised when he is accused of being a thief by the king's guards when they see him pulling the horse.

Obatalá tries to explain that he did not want to steal the horse but instead tries to return the lost animal to its true owner. The situation is confusing. The soldiers threaten him with spears as if he were a thief. Without allowing him to speak, he is arrested along with other real evildoers. Obatalá is silenced in prison for all the pain and misfortunes he has suffered. He is dismayed on the floor, remembering everything that had been prevented and regretting not having done the recommended advice and not having waited a few more days before starting the trip. Looking at the sky, he contemplates the extensive power of his reign, understanding the consequences of his eagerness.

Seven years passed (the magical number of creation) and the land of Shangó was torn between poverty and despair. His people died from the dryness, and a lack of rain turned the soil into barren land with small crops. Livestock cattle and sterility made life succumb little by little.

The fortune-tellers appeared before their King, saying:

*—We have consulted the Orishás. They say that a very wise and power-
ful old man was unjustly imprisoned and that such an act of injustice
has made us worthy of all the misfortunes in your kingdom.*

Shangó consults the jail guards and orders them to bring the old
man who was in prison for exactly 7 years. The old man, trembling as
he walks, hunched over, but with great dignity and peace, makes his way
among the people, who, seeing the halo of light that surrounds him, de-
parts with respect. His clothes are still impeccable and white as if time
had not passed. When approaching Shangó, Yemayá recognizes him and
gives a cry of exclamation:

—You are Obatalá!

Distressed by the emotion, she asks for his blessing while drops of
sea spill out of her eyes. Oshún experiences the same joy and, while
kissing the hands of Yemayá, breaks in a cry of joy and her tears make
the dry rivers grow.

Naná Burukú goes out to meet him and bows to his presence, saying:

*—May the rain cleanse all traces of possible dirt, sorrows, or regrets that
you, beloved Obatalá, have had suffered.*

And every drop that fell on his body became a bud that began to
germinate in the fields.

As he approached his father, Shangó prostrated at his feet, asking for
forgiveness for everything he had to go through due to his negligence
and lack of knowledge. He knew that he was the world, that his power
encompassed everything, that if his father suffered or had thirst or hunger,
others would also suffer. And as a demonstration of love and respect, all
the people who remained on their knees before Orixalá (the maximum
of the Orishás), slowly and under the orders of Shangó, began to gather
water from rain and the river. The waters, collected in large earthenware
vessels, were placed around him as a tribute and offering.

This is known in Candomblé as "the waters of Oxalá" and it's part
of the rituals commemorating this Patakkí.

10. Ofún | *Ten open seashells and six closed*

"Where the curse comes from."

The time has come to concretize and realize things. It is time for your most anticipated projects to have real bases and be carried out. Do not ignore the circumstances that may appear and that may interfere with your plans.

It's important to quickly materialize the things you want to achieve so that your interest or the need that motivated you doesn't fade away. The conviction and force of execution are the fundamental tools to prepare your future plans or meet urgent needs that have to do with the present.

Keep in mind that to achieve your objectives, they must be well prepared and based on reason and good direction.

Do not insist on the impossible or on whims. Stubbornness can take you through bad roads.

Difficult paths will keep you away from your goals. These are very insecure situations such as the fantasizing idealization with which you approached similar circumstances that made you lose valuable time in the past and is now irretrievable.

You should know that what is safe has firm and real bases that can materialize. If you try hard and put your skills into practice, everything will have a good ending.

Insisting on inaction and stubbornness can only create delay and you could possibly lose hope.

The effort should be your noblest tool and you will have to put it into practice in any task.

If you notice or someone makes you realize that adversity walks by your side, don't hesitate to change course. A turn in attitude or action could save you.

If you believe that you have been cursed or bewitched to change your luck, turn to the power of the Orishás (or any other technique based on High White Magic) and go forward without looking back or to your sides. Just watch your back, protect yourself, and continue your work.

Do not do the same as your victimizers. Do not raise your hand to point or your voice to curse.

Allow your feet and your mind to be fast and efficient. Walk and don't stop. Continue and persevere. If you don't know the path where you are traveling, don't worry, because someone else has already traveled that road and will be waiting for you upon arrival to accompany and guide you correctly.

If you are under a curse, you would carry disease and your energy field would be blocked. To avoid it, focus on the spiritual.

Mobilize your energies, put them into operation, and then follow carefully the indications of those who know this subject.

Do not neglect your Orishás (if it is part of your religion). If you are not part of it but have universal concepts that allow you a mental breadth, ask the good superior energies to protect you on your way and ask for protection from your guardian angel.

Finally, invoke the protection of Almighty God and he will hear it. Do not doubt a single moment.

Don't lose faith in your projects; link the spiritual with the material without forgetting that the spiritual and the material cannot be separated.

By establishing this right balance, you will not have to worry about the origin of the "curses" because you will be shielded against any attack and completely protected from the harassment of your enemies.

Patakkí

Ofún, wise and great magician who lived in ancient Africa, focused on the study of the deep arts that communicated him to the world of the spirits that gave him power and knowledge.

The story tells that since very small, Ofún had a reserved nature and that instead of entertaining himself with typical games of his age, he preferred to go deep into the dense jungle, away from everyone and away from the houses, in search of peace and tranquility. Taking refuge in his rich inner world, he began his daily task in search of the spiritual.

Ofún began the mornings by extending his arms to the sun and, in a very respectful way, he asked that on that day he would also be deserving of receiving all its energy and vitality. He did the same with the moon, to which he spoke muttering almost in a secret way.

Despite his young age, Ofún became a powerful wizard. He was able to mentally talk to animals with whom he had an intense attraction. His world was the occult arts and his destiny was the paranormal. His mission in life was the "hidden arts."

As to all being endowed, he was greatly hurt by the incomprehension of others, which made him suffer too much. For this reason he chose to live alone. Despite feeling always accompanied by invisible things that cannot be perceived by ordinary people, over the years he began to feel the need to be accompanied because loneliness was already affecting him.

Already at an advanced age, he considered that it was too late to get married and chose to educate and raise the children of less affluent families. Fortunate children received housing, food, affection, and a broad education. He prepared those he considered suitable for the functions of medium and for the complex but at the same time fascinating world of magic. To all of them he said:

—*Everything that is covered is forbidden to the eyes of the curious.*

And then he carefully covered all his magic tools with a white sheet with fine embroidery. Among them was an important book of one hundred pages of potions, enchantments, and other powerful tools.

Every day early in the morning he went to the jungle to talk to the spirits. The souls of the birds guided him and the egunes (the souls of the dead that inhabit certain sacred trees) helped him with his charms. Before leaving for the jungle, he recommended to his pupils that they had to take good care of the house and not allow strangers to enter. He said that caution was synonymous with security and that it's always prudent to distrust those we do not know well. Above all, he told them that under any circumstance they couldn't uncover what was under the white mantle.

In those days, a little girl named Annanagu lived with him. The girl's parents had left her under Ofún's care because they could not support her or offer her education. The girl was gaining the love of her protector who soon perceived her attributes and chose her as his disciple. Annanagu learned that above all things, respect, perseverance and understanding were essential.

Annanagu incorporated into her apprenticeship the essential teaching that all things eventually arrived at the exact moment, neither before nor after, and to the correct extent. Even though there might be obstacles, no one in this world could stop what was karmatically determined for a person.

The love and respect between teacher and student reached such a point that Annanagu's parents began to mistrust the "sorcerer" maliciously. They began to suspect that behind the mysterious curtain existed great treasures that were controlled by powerful forces responsible for the submission of the will of his daughter to the great and lonely Ofún.

One day very early in the morning, Annanagu's parents waited carefully until the magician left the house and headed for the plants and trees, making sure he could no longer see them. Then, they entered stealthily in the house, taking advantage of the absence of Ofún, and surprised the girl who was scared to see her parents in the house unexpectedly. Without talking to her and with intimidation and gestural threats, her parents cornered her until they told her that if she did not show them what her teacher hid behind the curtain, they had no choice but to kidnap her and take her away from the magician and her teachings. She would never see him again.

The girl began to cry with despair and, between sobs, tried to make them reconsider. Remembering the sorcerer's words with a certain tone of security, she told her parents:

—*All that is covered is forbidden to the eyes of the curious.*

Her parents laughed and mocked her, and with a quick and abrupt jerk, they opened the curtain that separated the living room from the room where Ofún performed his magic.

The magician's spirits alerted him that something was disturbing the tranquility in his house and he quickly started to return. As he approached he heard the cries and the tears of the girl. Concerned, he entered the house saw the girl's parents trying to remove the mantle. He immediately took Annanagu away while comforting and telling her that it was not her fault.

The girl's parents fled in shame and terror at seeing the strange light as bright and powerful as the sun itself. When running, terror seized them and due to the strong light, they lost sight for a while. Their spiritual ignorance made them believe that their momentary blindness had been caused by the curses of Ofún that Annanagu had told them.

Their ignorance and the outrage committed, in addition to their bad feelings and greed, had been responsible for their wrong doings. Nothing else had harmed them. And, the eyes of the curious could not see.

11. Ojuani | *Eleven open seashells and five closed*

"Transporting water with a straw basket is not very profitable."

The little practicality and the repetition of already proven and known errors leads to disaster. It's like turning your head to ignore reality.

There are two shortcuts, one uphill with stones in its path and the other one is bordering the hillside and is clear of debris. You have already traveled the first one and already know it. You walked barefoot and got to your destination with bleeding feet and it took you a long time to arrive. You're not familiar with the second shortcut, but you know that it is smooth, flat, and will take you where you want to go.

Confusion in states of consciousness can make you choose the wrong path, and this decision would only bring you pain and uncertainty.

To insist on repeating old mistakes without accepting necessary changes and without changing behaviors would be an unthinking and hostile attitude against yourself.

If there are dark shadows that blind your judgment and you do nothing to remove them, you will end up becoming a shadow as well. You will be part of them and then it may be too late to escape and find the light.

Ask Elegguá to allow you to clear your path and remove those shadows that are nothing but the spirits of the compulsive dead (*Kiumbas*). Ask Oyá to set them apart.

To heal your bleeding wounds, invoke Babaluaie with strength and passion in your requests and with resignation during the time for recovery. Do not be violent or argue angrily, as you may incur in pitiful quarrels, otherwise you might end up doing what the enemies intend you to do.

Don't think about your enemies; forget about them completely. Ask for light for their souls and minds. This will help them to forget about you, and little by little they'll drop their hostile attitude.

If you failed to raise water, accept it and you will see how the water that fell on the earth made the arid land disappear.

When failures, defeats, and mistakes are admitted, we will have taken the initial step to consciously start all we want to undertake.

Modify your actions and have hope because it is essential to have faith in what you execute.

Trust yourself and in others who want to collaborate demonstrating good will and good feelings.

Give yourself an opportunity by believing in your abilities and trusting in the strength of God, in his Supreme Justice, in his repairing laws and plans. Through them and with your effort, you can change what seems unchangeable.

This letter refers to the repetition and/or modification of facts or things, or the ability to transform them into completely different ones.

This is the reason why the Ashé of Oshumaré appears framing the sky with its bright colors and uses its rainbow as a bridge between earth and sky for those who can modify their erroneous behaviors with the strength of the will, foreseeing the spiritual ascent and the ability to transmute their karma.

In this case, the content and meaning of this Odú brings sagacity, cunning, and knowledge as well as enough seduction to move with comfort and fullness.

Patakkí

Once a year all the saints met in the palace of Orumilá to listen to their stories full of great power and mysticism.

When the saints were received in the palace, with only the first exchange of words and with incredible precision, Orumilá told them everything that had happened to them during the year. Still wanting to confuse him, Orumilá always got his way and offered the most accurate details.

Everyone wondered how it was possible that without leaving his house, Orumilá knew absolutely everything that happened to them, including the things that happened in their kingdoms or to themselves.

Everyone got together, determined to reveal such an important secret, and came to the conclusion that everyone was going through exactly the same thing. Although they always tried to have the utmost reserve and the utmost care in ensuring that nothing came to Orumilá's ears, nothing escaped him. The intrigued Orishás spoke with great anxiety trying to plan how to unveil the mystery that surrounded the fortune-teller.

Eshú, who was sitting behind the door, listened attentively without missing any detail and without giving any opinion. Looking at Eshú, Oshún asked him:

—*What's your opinion, owner of the roads and crossroads? What do you know or think about it?*

Someone else asked:

—*You may be able to help us and tell us which way to go, or what to do to find out about Orumilá's secrets.*

Eshú answered:

—*Maybe I can help you, but keep in mind that by now, in this moment, Orumilá already knows what you are planning and he knows exactly all the details. I think the most correct thing to do would be to ask him and accept his answer as true. We all know that there are many secrets that cannot be revealed.*

They agreed and decided to go to see Orumilá to ask him the technique he used, and how it was possible that he always knew everything.

Later they went to see him. When they approached and surrounded him, with great respect, they one by one asked about his abilities.

Orumilá listened to them carefully and then told them:

—*Everything I am and have, everything that I represent, I owe to my board. Through its use I get things.*

He finished his answer and didn't say anything else. Then he waited for their reaction. Shangó spoke:

—*But your answer is vague and not as precise as your verdicts are. Actually, it's not what we're expecting*

—*That is my answer, real and true.*

And with dignified gestures, he waited for the consent of all the Orishás.

At the end of the meeting, Eshú told the fortune-teller everything and left him surprised and worried at the same time.

Having not been very satisfied with the answer, they met again to analyze what Orumilá had said. They came to the conclusion that he evidently could know everything, but that surely would keep him very busy. How could he have the rest of his things so orderly, like his palace and belongings? How did he get his food? How did he cure his ailments?

After all these musings, they decided to give him a test. He had to heal a mortal who had long suffered from a strange disease. Surely he could do it thanks to his great knowledge, because apparently, everything was in his power.

Eshú told Orumilá everything that was discussed and planned after the meeting. Orumilá answered:

—*My answer was the truth Eshú! You know very well that I have the gift of prophecy and not healing. However, and in spite of everything, we will win this bet!*

You and I will be inseparable, and without being asked, the man will be completely cured of his illness. Thus, they will have to accept that not everything can be told and that what they planned is unsuccessful. It's as useless as wanting to catch the water with a bottomless container.

I can know what illness afflicts that man and you will help me undo it. Our alliance will be invincible. We will be unconditional allies to such an extent that your spirit will live on my board and will have a place of preeminence.

The land of many roads has been gathered and once cursed, they bewitched him with the earth and other things. Yes, that's what the mortal is really suffering. Who better than you, the owner of the crossroads, to retrace the path of those who wanted to make him sick and undo the spell! Walk one by one all the roads that walked those who did so much harm to this poor and innocent creature to make him sick completely. And who better than I, the owner of all the Oracles, to determine the type of ebó to follow!

Soon, the man healed completely and he announced it everywhere.

To each kingdom came the news, which left all the Orishás totally amazed. Not only had Orumilá already learned of their plans, but surely he had also been the one who healed the man. None of them had managed to cure the man before because they could not pinpoint where the disease was. Then they decided to make a big party as compensation and to celebrate they went to look for Orumilá and brought him all kinds of food and drinks for the entertainment.

Orumillá told them:

—*You can see how you give me big banquets without leaving my palace. And all this I owe exclusively to my divination board.*

And addressing Eshú, he said:

—And since this is my home and I want you to take care of my paths, I invite you, Eshú, to be the one who starts the evening by tasting your favorite dishes.

And that's the way it was and will continue to be. Eshú received and will always receive his meals first as a reward for his work.

12. Eyila Chebora | *Twelve open seashells and four closed*

"Wake up, otherwise you will lose the war. Courage will be your ally!" "Be orderly and not restless or unruly, otherwise and in spite of everything, they will manage to defeat you."

If the consultant is a man, he will have great possibilities of "having a head" of Shangó. That is, this Orishá could be his Guardian Angel. If the consultant is a woman, it is most likely that her Orishá is Oshún or Oyá.

In both cases, the consultant will find his/her partner in the person who has a head in one of the referred saints. For example, if your partner its a man, he would have to have "Shangó's head."

You have a very strong sense of justice, and for this reason there are those who freely declare your enemies even without you knowing them or knowing of their existence.

The respect you have for courage and audacity do not have to tip you to war. You will have other weapons that are not precisely weapons of war to defend the just. Always be alert in any action. Do not neglect your weak sides; be prudent and orderly and you will win easily.

You must reject the aggression, whether verbal, physical, or of any kind. Your struggle should focus on other values. You will be fully trained for it.

When you control your character, which can often be presented as irrational or explosive, you would contribute to peace and permanent equilibrium.

You are the kind of person who is recognized by phrases such as: "He or she has a heart of gold," or "People can ask you to do anything in a good way."

This is true if people manage to approach you in good manners, with good intentions and on good terms. In general, you are willing to help others, which reflects your fraternal and community spirit.

If they approach you with lies, belittlements, haughtiness, arrogance, or attempts to cut off the freedom of others, your reaction could be quite irritable and sometimes violent.

Remember, even if the cause was justified, you must weigh your sense of balance, avoiding bursting into screams or arguments that can bring serious consequences in those moments. By following the advice of the letter, there will be no storm in the sky that can intimidate you.

Do not fear, the voice of Shangó's thunder only stuns those who are not noble at heart and deadens the treacherous and disloyal by repressing the action of injustice.

Advance and do not allow recoil. Even advancing twice as much as you backtrack, there will always be a balance that is not positive (some delay), although the balance may seem otherwise. Accept the advice of your elders who have already walked the path in the past. Keep in mind that they may be the only ones you can trust.

There will be many people who will approach you to confuse you with flattery and cordial gestures while they are shielded with studied movements that hide vested interests far removed from the true feelings.

Even when you recognize them for their false performance, and despite helping them in whatever they need, you will always be criticized. You represent what they, inflamed by jealousy and envy, can never achieve because of their spiritual and mental narrowness.

It would be advisable that you only surround yourself with people who appreciate you for what you are as a human being and for your values, and not people who over time show that they are ephemeral and interested only in what you may have today, encompass, or represent.

The environment of a human being is very important. It is the lung that enables breathing, making its life viable. Being surrounded by positive things, from people who love you, care about you, and want the best for you even at the expense of your own interests, is like having half the way to go in your favor. The rest of the path will be easier to cover.

Patakkí

All the seers had gathered in an ancient kingdom. They were concerned about the lack of elephant tusks that were much needed in various divination implements.

They consulted the oracles and determined that the task could only be carried out by brave men with a healthy heart and a noble temper. Tusks should be obtained without mistreating the animal. The one who could do it that way would be the legitimate and worthy successor to the throne.

The king, who was already very old, entrusted the task to his son, Moderiko, who was not much loved or respected by the people for having a reckless, violent, and irrational character.

Addressing Moderiko, the king said:

—*Son, you would have to be my heir on the throne and that would be my wish and your right by bloodline. But the fortune-tellers of the kingdom say that only the one who catches an elephant without making it suffer will be my successor.*

I know you're violent and you desire war, so I think it's impossible for you to hunt the animal in that way. However, I'm asking you as a sovereign and as your father. I do not want to die without seeing that you really deserve to wear my crown.

But remember, as the king, I always governed with peace and without violence, trying to be as fair as possible and giving my people the best of me to live in full harmony. I ask you to take this mission as a test of heaven, as I really believe it is. Maybe this is not a test just for you, but also for me for not being strict with you and for not being able to channel or control your character.

The king showed that he was really sad and worried. Years of work and dedication to his people were adrift and without a clear future. He did not trust his son's abilities, but he was also upset at the idea that a stranger could take his place. The only thing that calmed him down was the thought that whoever was going to be the next king, that person should have a noble and just heart.

The first reaction of Moderiko was to go out into the jungle with all his hunting gear, in search of his prey. He spent several days in the jungle and remembered his father's words each second. For him, they were torturing, demanding, too strict, severe, and contradictory to his nature and temperament. He was so preoccupied and absorbed in his thoughts that he had not realized that for several days he had been followed by a group of criminals whom were trying to obstruct his plans.

Finally, exhausted and very worried about not knowing what to do to avoid the king's disappointment, Moderiko lay down on the grass to rest. When he woke up the next day, he saw with astonishment that his bow had disappeared and his arrows were broken at his side. At first he thought it had been the work of some thief, but then he realized that behind all that there was something more important and that would probably have to do with the inheritance of the throne. Hurriedly, he returned to the palace and publicly told what happened.

When he finished telling what had happened, all the assistants testified that a few days before his arrival, a man from the village had claimed the victory after hunting a large prey, but that the final word had not yet been said on how he had achieved it, and there were certain flaws and doubts. The fortune-tellers had not yet met to entrust details to the king about the feat accomplished by this man.

The next day there was a great uproar in the palace. Everyone ran from one side to the other because in a few minutes it would be known if the heir was already chosen or not. Among the fortune-tellers there was the oldest of all, who had arrived in the kingdom a few days before. The fortune-teller stood up and, respectfully addressing the king, said:

—*Deceit and not the nobility of the soul is who wanted to seize the crown.*

I challenge the impostor who, taking advantage of the fact that your son was sleeping, seized his things and then killed the elephant but made a mistake in his desire for power.

I invite you, and there is no doubt that you have killed the animal, to demonstrate convincingly that you were not the one with all these tricks who tried to achieve what your heart can not reach.

Show us another of your arrows that you say they're yours, because it is well known that every hunter has several arrows with its personal marks and other secrets that only the owner recognizes.

The imposter could not respond or show anything. The wise old man continued saying:

—Moderiko, take a step forward please. Could you instead show us another arrow like the one that hurt and finally killed the animal? But before that, if you're so kind, could you describe it to us?

The king's son described step by step every detail of his arrows, its size, the type of wood, the shape of the arrow's head, and the symbolic inscriptions that belonged to him. The description was exactly the same as the arrow that was held by the fortune-teller's consul. Then, opening one of his hunter's bags, the wise man removed what was left of one of the arrows, and searched through the pieces until he could finally assemble it.

The old fortune-teller, addressing the king, said:

—Your son, my lord, has shown dignity, respect for your person, honesty, and willingness to comply with the designations marked by the oracle. His delay in the jungle was due to the time it took him to decide how to hunt such an animal without hurting it seriously and without making it suffer with his hands.

He waited, controlled his instincts, sacrificed his impulses, and tempered his spirit, knowing that it could cost him the kingdom. Deep in respect, he waited for Divine inspiration, trusting that it would come in some way if he were worthy of such a noble hierarchy.

Without knowing it, but intuitively, he patiently waited for the natural death of one of those animals and then could take away the precious material that was the indispensable condition in the test.

And addressing Moderiko, the old man continued:

—*Thanks to the piety you had, the patience, the respect for your elders and the kingdom, your people and the Deities, your heart was ennobled and, for the first time, you proved to have the necessary qualities to be a king.*

It was actually one of your arrows that managed to kill the elephant, but it was not your hands. The animal did not suffer because of your will or your choice. Your honesty was rewarded because everything we know and spread, we verify by the oracles.

Finally, looking at the king, the old man announced:

—*Majesty, your crown will be protected!*

13. Metanlá | *Thirteen open seashells and three closed*

"The illness comes from the sickness of the blood."

A vain and disrespectful man does not understand that the day needs the night; he forgets the stars and does not dare to look up to the sky.

To reject the balance of the opposites is to deny your own faculties and your own nature.

In a world made of different things, something that looks different could be more similar than our own reflection on the water.

The unequal is necessary to make us remember that sometimes reality could be the reflection of several things.

The sun and the fire could reflect identical or similar shadows, however both energies are different, but for an instance, they seem to have the same purposes: providing heat, dynamism, and vitality.

Whatever is too far away from you is also very close to your inner self. Don't look too far away, because sometimes the answers we cannot find are closer than we think. We only have to learn to recognize and accept them.

Forgetting these principles and not venerating what supports life is when a person with weak character, compulsive and discriminatory, attracts sickness and emptiness, drought and barrenness, and infertility and death.

Respect for your life does not include the submission of your body to destructive excess. It includes taking care of the matter that houses your spirit, its conservation, support, maintenance, and cleanliness.

The mind should not be forgotten. As an intermediary between your body and spirit, it deserves the same care.

And finally, your soul, that's the unmistakable engine that allows everything else, must be a rise in the spiritual development.

The abuses committed against someone bring sadness, pain, and sorrow.

What is considered death, kisses and embraces warmly in an instance to what is considered life. They look like opposites, but instead, they're just momentary lapses in different planes of existence. They both need each other to continue their existence and meet different cycles.

Your obligation is to meet what you have committed to do in other planes even if you don't remember it.

This promise is related to self-respect and respect for your life here on earth. Only when you take care of the integrity and proper functioning of your health will you be assuring is permanency in this planet allowing your spirit to evolve and repair its own faults through reincarnation.

The same fault, or perhaps even a more serious error, is to push others to follow destructive paths. In that case, you would be assuming a bigger responsibility restricting other's freedom. The message involves the respect for all and all the things that God has placed on earth. We shall not make a distinction among human beings, discriminate, or reject in advance what we don't understand or is different, without having a valid and fair reason.

Ask for a total vision of things, for an open and harmonized mind, a spiritual outlook that includes love and fraternity as the main purpose. Ask also for the revaluation of the body, mind, and spirit.

This is the Odú used by Omulú, Babaluallé (also known as Xapaná, Chapaná, Shapaná, or Obaluaié), owner of ajá, and he shakes it and slaps it on the air to reject impurities and illnesses.

Like the number that rules this Odú (related to the karma), many times it's feared and rejected and it's been responsible for all the fear represented for the number thirteen. It's not considered as a possibility for reparation because it's enlightening and has the opportunity to teach.

The duality that covers the number thirteen (concepts based more on superstition than reality) bring a double message: confusion and also the image of this beloved Orishá. For many that misinterpreted the message, it represents the cause for sickness and also almost the one that provokes illness. In fact, these concepts are wrong and far from reality.

I think these mistakes are not intentional but are the result of lack of information and the fear that many humans have toward illness. It's also the rejection of positive or negative things around themselves. It's like denying (lacking the willingness of seeing, listening, or knowing anything) what it takes to recover or how he or she got sick in the first place.

Babaluallé cures the illnesses, protects the sick, alleviates the grieving, eradicates the sickness, fights viruses, and if this was not enough, finds solutions throughout the inspiration of the mediums for cures, discoveries, and many other ways to fight sickness. This is a noble action that influences the mind of scientists, doctors, and everyone that has a sacred mission to cure the sick.

He's well known as the "doctor for the poor" and his role is that of a high benefactor. He's begged for the healing and recovery from all illnesses, whether psychic, spiritual, or corporeal.

Patakkí

Babaluallé, coming from Yoruba land, finally is crowned as the high priest and governor in the land of Dahomey. Next to his mother, Naná Burukú, they become two of the most adore, and respected deities of their culture.

The legends say that at the beginning of life in the planet, Babaluallé was one of the first Orishás that started living and getting closer to humans, and little by little, started to forget his divine origin. He was living a chaotic life, perhaps on decadence, and had many women as lovers at the same time. Ignoring the advice from other Orishás to abandon his disorderly life, even Olofi (God Almighty) aware of what was going on, imposed a great test:

—*You should not have sexual relationships on Holy Thursday.*

And the order came from the infinite space.

Despite that the day was approaching, he forgets what Olofi had ordered and falls once again to temptation. When he feels disregard for others after what had happened, he goes from town to town, from village to village, without the same act of celebration and festivity he was used to, but now with loneliness, lack of appreciation, and experience of the same kind of sickness that affects humans.

His character changes, and little by little he turns introspective, reserved, and shy, and his personality changes. He becomes more sensible, and without knowing if a result of self-punishment for his faults or because the pain that he feels due human sickness, he starts to experience epidemic outbreaks on his skin. Wounds and sores, red marks, spots, and damages leave footprints like scars on his skin. Everybody ignores him and nobody talks to him. Sad and ashamed, he covers all his body so nobody can see his illness.

Sick and lonely, Babaluallé continues his path, until Eshú appears (as Ifá's messenger) and advises him to retire to another land. Babaluallé agrees and from then on he would turn into the sovereign of another village. Eshú tells him:

—*You will cure the men as an order from Olofi.*

Babaluallé accepts and walks next to his dog (a gift from Ogún). Under the Catholic aspect, he's known as Saint Roch or Saint Rocco. When he gets to the new kingdom, his mother, Naná Burukú acknowledges that her son has fulfilled his mission curing many people and reduced the pain on the defenseless without worrying if he has to suffer from their illnesses. She intercedes before God and asks him if the water could cure her son.

Once Naná gets to Dahomey's land, she makes raindrops fall over her son. The first drops that touch him sterilize his wounds and the last ones cure him completely. When the people see the miracle, he is crowned their king. Once again, the voice from the oracle speaks.

14. Merinlá | *Fourteen open seashells and two closed*

"Be fair and measured, without doing more or less, but fair and impartial."

A fair human being recognizes the changes in nature because he lives in harmony with it and creates bonds that will last. He's more in-tune with balances and energetic compensations. He knows that when the sun is out and it rains, a rainbow would shine in the sky. He knows how to wait and knows his time.

He accepts when the sun rises because he believes in perfect synchronism and waits once again with new hopes when the conditions permit.

The wise man knows that everything is a form of compensation, and in the balance of things, is manifested just and accurate. It's not worth it to come early. Following behind brings detriment.

The exact time is correct because it brings the right action on the expansive movements of the letter. Not before, not later, just within and at the same time. This is the right way to execute an action. To recognize the changes, even the elusive ones, identify the wise and just men.

The wise men adjust to the times and get ready for what's coming; distributing their values correctly, fortifying their houses, straighten their moral values. And what's more important, respecting everybody's soul.

Getting ready for the future will overcome difficult times. Believing in life in times to come will ratify your beliefs on evolution and the regeneration of things.

Act with justice and the right balance—no more, no less.

You won't be asked to give more than you can, and you won't ask for less than you really need. In this way, you will get the right amount of things to help you plan for today and tomorrow.

To value the present should be an order coming from your inner self to be able to structure the bases needed to plan the future and foresee changes that could cause unrest. This could be your best and successful approach to different aspects of life.

Patakkí

Olodumaré had declared the creation of the world with the intention that, in the future, Earth would be capable of incarnating millions and millions of souls, and after acquiring physical bodies through the Reincarnation Law, they could evolve spiritually every time.

According to some stories, it was Obatalá (or Oxalá) who was in charge of carrying out this mission under the Supreme Creator mandate whom gave him a sack. The divine sack contained powerful and magical energies that were able to interact with each other forming avspiral of forces. When the energies blended, always rotating on the same axis, it emitted rays of light that created dense energy particles forming basic matter.

Tired and thirsty, Obatalá drank until his thirst was quenched. Eshú didn't have good intentions and placed on the road several bottles of wine of palm to tempt Obatalá, as a result of previous quarrels they had with each other. Obatalá fell deeply asleep and when he woke up he found out that the sack of creation had disappeared. His brother, Oddudduá, had stolen it. (In other versions, the story is represented by the female version of Obatalá.)

This is the way Yoruba people explain the mythological rivalry that exists between brothers in many cultures, like the biblical concept of Cain and Abel. Or, it could explain more precisely the historic fact the Igbó Kingdom (later on transformed into the city of Ifé) was lost after a military battle directed by Oddudduá, which took away the reign from Obatalá (also known as Orishá Igbó) because he was the King of the Igbós.

From that moment on, Olodumaré prohibits Obatalá to drink wine of palm (as we just saw in another story), and instead of the soil that was inside the magic sack stole by Oddudduá, gave him a kind of clay to mold humankind.

In another version related to the drinking prohibition, Obatalá begins to mold humans in a careless way without giving importance to the restriction imposed by his father. As a consequence of this action, we see malformations and defects, and different skin tones because the molds have been removed from the cooking oven before time.

This was how albinos were created in the first place, and they belong to the ruling Orishá. There is no need to "mark them with a Saint" (a mark through the sacred reading of seashells, or which is his or her ruling Orishá) because all of them are direct children of Obatalá.

From these stories, Obatalá is known as the owner of all heads because he is in charge of attaching them to the rest of the human body.

15. Marunlá | *Fifteen open seashells and one closed*

"You can use the path to walk on or stop. On the path you could follow or be followed. You can walk or stop, however, it will always be a path."

Irritability leads to destruction and absurd war.

There should never be a fight among brothers, and children should never incur in the greatest of abuses to their parents: oblivion.

He who forgets his parents not only does not remember them, but does not love them.

Their image should be always in our hearts, in our feelings.

To abandon these values brings a lack of affection, suffering, and darkness for the soul.

Such a wrong action brings a whirlwind of negativities and a spiritual fall.

To forget those who gave us life and brought us to this world is like not being aware of what can take us away from it.

Anyone who has been blessed with the sacred roll of parenthood must follow these concepts very closely.

The mere sexual act of procreation does not, by itself, assign the hierarchy of these conceptual values.

It's necessary much more and could be resumed in one word: love.

Love is such an immense feeling for the parents that even the most difficult challenges and furious reactions turn everything into examples and lessons to form, correct and channel life.

The man will appease the woman and vice versa when any of them offend their parents. Who does that will be a good husband or wife and finally a good parent.

The mission of the partner will be to encourage him/her to continue and amend the wrong things, overcoming the difficulties in pursuit of the union.

The deep message of the letter is to urge the family union without altering the natural order of the cycles, striving for everything to unfold in harmony and tranquility.

Love will always unite us, and nothing that has been created by love can be destroyed.

To appease the violent emotions, to put off the violence, and to discard resentments and move our hearts from anger that only brings obfuscation and doom, are the messages (and no others) of the letter. The letter also advises in every instant the strength of the unit.

After achieving the unification that gives the solidity of the union, we will surpass the calm, the tensions will decrease, and the peace will reign.

If it is difficult to find a solution for all of this because of life circumstances out of your control. Have a good thought, do not keep grudges, remember the positive, and above all, know how to forgive. Raise your thought to God and ask for light and protection for all and you will have peace of mind. You will have done everything possible to establish harmony in your life and in the life of others.

Patakki

At the beginning of time, when men held great parties dedicated to the Orishás, in the midst of the preparations and projects of festivities, great terror invaded the hearts of the organizers.

When almost everything was in progress and about to begin with each of the honorees, immense waves emerged from the sea. Deafening roars seemed to come out of the ocean while their waters flooded all around dragging to their immensities all the things that appeared in front of its path.

Before the astonished gaze of many, the majestic figure of Yemayá could be seen high up on the crest of the waves. At that time almost everyone remembered that the only Orishá who had not been prepared nor organized any celebration in his/her honor was only the great mother of all the other Deities (except those of Dahomean origin, which are believed to come from of another mother: Naná Burukú).

The matriarchal figure and unmistakable hierarchy of the great mother of the waters had been seriously offended.

Embraced and sad at the time of being forgotten by her children, she commanded swirling water that destroyed everything. Its waters were so riotous that they gave the appearance of being of dark color, which reflected the bitterness and the affliction of Yemayá.

Desperate men begged for the protection of the King of Peace, Obatalá, whom they knew as the only one who could soothe and pacify her completely. So he raised his *paxoró* of silver, his great staff loaded with deep and powerful mysticism (the symbol with which he presides over the world). With a gesture of infinite magnificence, he ordered the halting of the waters and put an end to such a sweeping scene.

The sparkling, silver and-white lights flashed from his immaculate scepter into the deepest parts of the ocean. Right there, as if coming out of a great hypnotic trance, Yemayá understood that despite such a great offense, its waters could not and should not destroy the creation of Oxalá. The waters quieted down immediately. The deafening noise stopped and everything returned to harmony and regained its natural and translucent color.

With the same staff that had served to separate the world from the Deities and from Humankind, Oxalá restored normalcy, and peace reigned again.

16. Merindiloggún | *Sixteen open seashells*

"A wise man is the one who knows how to listen, and a good ruler knows how to respect the requests and needs of his people. The wise governs the heads of all and does not ignore the ancestral voice of the oracle."

To listen, to silence, and to see, in time, is to ignore, to speak, and to close the eyes when it is necessary. It all depends on the circumstances and the facts that surround us.

Only the one who is enlightened is prepared to really see, to speak with the truth, and to listen to the most hidden sounds.

Those who survive the power of silence and endure the continuity of the agile thoughts of psychic order can manage the power of the verb and the word.

The one who listens most will be the one who can speak more properly at the right time. The one who speaks less, the better he can refute. And whoever sees "the real" of things can see what other eyes can not see, even what goes beyond the material.

You will be able to perceive with total clarity the invisible things that are in this dimension and those that do not belong to this world.

Your gaze will seem lost on the horizon, but you will really have found the path of eternity without borders sharpening your resources of perception and increasing your power.

Do not be afraid to look further. There are lands and places unsuspected by many men. They are places that tomorrow will be kept as expressions of longings and desires of good fortune.

Even if you cannot touch them, they are there and they will continue to be as you open your heart. Only the man who looks with the heart captures reality.

If they do not understand or share your thoughts, do not throw them away or abandon them, just go far enough so you do not get hurt.

Let them experience for themselves and if they fail to discover the truth of the spirit, it will not be yet their time or their hour.

This letter brings peace and happiness. You are protected and blessed by Orishála. Wear white in his honor so his vibration will easily reach you.

Good business and prosperity will knock on your door.

Learning was not in vain because you didn't ask for more or offer less. The balance of the action of living is offered as the reward after an arduous path

The lessons were incorporated as something that was latent and only needed to wake you up.

You are really trained to lead and guide many people. Many people need you and expect your word and advice. These people trust in what you do and believe in your word. You have people who are waiting and need you.

The coronation will come, and when this happens, you will be prepared. Then it will be the moment when you can give each one according to what their needs require, and their spiritual conditions allow.

No one can take what is yours. Get ready to meet people on your way who will envy your skills.

Do not worry, because your path is traced and guided by a huge and powerful spiritual light that protects you even from those from the dark who think themselves powerful.

You have visionary and prophetic gifts, hands that will alleviate the pain, and a heart that will love without conditions.

All these beautiful things would be reserved for you. Only give it time to mature with the teachings, learn from the sacrifice, and overcome the stages with pride and dignity, and the reward will be enormous.

Patakkí

In the early days of Ilé Ifé (the ancestral and religious city of the Yorubas, considered to be the epicenter of creation), a stranger from distant lands arrived in the city.

In spite of having great knowledge on herbalist and ritual magic, he had moved away from his own people for not being able to understand some phenomena in the world of the magic. These events today could be considered as paranormal, which he was accustomed to perceiving, but his logical rationality prevented him from explaining.

Finding Ilé Ifé, a land of peace with an enormous spirituality reflected in each of its inhabitants, he felt comfortable and decided to settle in this place.

Otá was the name of this wise man, and among his qualities were fraternity, hypersensitivity, and his gifts as a medium. In addition to his numerous studies, he had an atmosphere of captivating mystery, and day after day his fame and popularity grew.

One day the king's daughter became seriously ill. The sovereign unhesitatingly broke into Otá's house, begging him desperately to heal his daughter. The Osainist (by that time he had become a great specialist in cures with plants, flowers, and herbs in general), remembering ancient rituals that he had never come to understand or rationalize, left his house as if something invisible dragged him from there. Staring at the sun, he implored it for its energy and vitality so that he could then transmit it to the sick woman, who at first sight lacked this energy.

Otá not only begged for the great magnetism of the sun, but also, in this test of fire imposed on him by life, he challenged the sun metaphorically by speaking and asking for absolute faith that he would never again need (to withdraw completely from torturous thoughts based more on logic than on spirituality).

With his arms outstretched and his gaze fixed on the sun, Otá tirelessly repeated the orders until a huge light embraced him. He immediately realized that it was time to act. Upon entering his house, he was blinded for a long time by the sun rays that were directly on his eyes. When he regained his vision, he sent the king's soldiers to bring the largest stone they could find, similar to the size and shape of the princess's figure. Then he placed the body of the patient on the stone and gradually began to sculpt her figure on it. This took several days to complete.

When he finished his work of art, he placed in parallel the two figures, the princess and the sculpture. He prepared *omiero* (a liquid used in various rituals) with herbs that he had ordered to be collected and gave it to the girl first to drink and then wet the carved lips on the stone that seemed to come to life. All were astonished when, almost at the same time, the two figures began to rise.

The princess ran to embrace her father and the stone stood up, standing in front of Otá. From the mouth of the perfect sculpture came these words:

—*Obá Otá.*

King of Stones.

And repeating this phrase several times, Olodumaré was heard addressing Otá from the immensity of the heavens, reaffirming a faith that he had almost lost. Otá lay down on the floor in a sign of respect and understood the significance of the signs, recognizing the importance of his mission.

The fame of Otá grew in the whole kingdom of the Yorubas, and his example was the basis and testimony of their beliefs.

Ramifications and Origins of the Odús

Through the combinations of the sixteen Odús, interrelated ramifications called *Orno Odú* are obtained. When multiplied and combined, they generate 256 responses until they reach 4,096 Odús. Among them, there are the so-called Major Odús (numbers 1, 2, 3, 4, 8, 10, 12, 13, 14, 15, and 16) and the Minor Odús (5, 6, 7, 9, and 11.)

The number 5, called Osé, is considered the smallest. The oldest is Owanní—Osé. Many of the legends are based on myths where various characters merged and played an important role and made possible the oral transmission of this knowledge through the centuries. They inspire reflection and bring together teachings and metaphors with conceptual clarity, investigating and penetrating the sociocultural world of any idiosyncrasy, however dissimilar the patterns that mobilize them.

Many of these Odús are born or originate from others. For these purposes it is necessary to know them and to manage these ramifications to perfection, so that when interrelating them, a total verdict is reached. In this way, each Odú is concomitantly united to another, of which it is a ramification and life at the same time, creating between them a perfect and just balance where feedback begins to occur.

When considering which letter was born from another, it is possible to obtain a more enlightening overall meaning and at the same time it is possible to compare it with the previous message when there were doubts due to lack of comparative concepts.

Each Odú is a reflection to make and take into account. It represents an oracle and symbolic thought that, through phrases and stories (often metaphorical), teach, prevent, and alert about spiritual, material, and moral situations.

It takes the contemplative ecstasy of a human–Orishá connection (Babalawo-Ifá) for Orumilá to respond and find true and practical representations in common and current language and to bring ancient teachings alive, which when adapting them to the rhythm of current societies, take effect and give timely premonitions.

Among the Yoruba in ancient Africa, the priests dedicated to Ifá (called Oluwos) were chosen from the time they were children and consecrated to him. These wise advisors, apart from having the rank of soothsayers, made their priesthood a kind of lifelong indoctrination where they continually channeled the mythical and sacred teachings, which their elders had conferred upon them.

From distant times to the present eras, they were the depositories of the eró (secret), and as my teachers said, they spoke with *Ifé ni okokán* (love and sweetness in the heart.)

We have already said that there are different names for each of the Odús. Also, between them, their meanings do not vary in spite of these differences in names. When we consult with the seashells, we often hear different names from the officiant. That does not matter or reveal any misconception on the part of the consultant.

Many of the oldest denominations fell into disuse and others, due to practice and use, became present and were adopted with greater acceptance.

Origins of the Odús

Odús	Origin
Okana	Comes From Ofún
Ejioko	Comes From Ejéunle
Ogundá	Comes From Odí
Iroso	Comes From Ojuani
Oché	Comes From Ejéunle
Obara	Comes From Eyila Chebora
Odí	Comes From Okana
Ejéunle	Comes From Merindiloggún
Osá	Comes From Odí

Ofún	Comes From Osá
Ojuani	Comes From Oché
Eyila Chebora	Comes From Ogundá
Metanlá	Comes From Oché And Ofún
Merinlá	Comes From Ejioko And Obara
Marunlá	Comes From Ejéunle And Osá
Merindiloggún	Comes From Ejéunle

In other words:

The №	Is Born of №
1	10
2	8
3	7
4	11
5	8
6	12
7	1
8	16
9	7
10	9
11	5
12	3
13	5 and 10
14	2 and 6
15	8 and 9
16	8

There is also a roll that is called Eyekún, also known as Opira and Adaké, and that is when all sixteen seashells fall with their closed side up. This combination is considered disastrous. Before continuing to consult, we must take fresh water in our hands and throw it above our head toward the ceiling as if wanting to dissipate the bad influence of this roll with water in the form of rain.

And as the beginning and the end seem to come together in the cycle of life, this important combination of chaos and confusion returns after its action at the beginning (the number 1.) This is the moral or proverb that accompanies this letter: "Your eyes are blindfolded, you are like blind and you can not see anything."

Proverbs for Double Configuration

These sayings and morals that often metaphorically highlight a whole system of symbolism should be interpreted when consulting twice in a row with the Diloggún. For example, if you have consulted with the sixteen cowrie shells, first the number 4 and then the number 6, you should refer to the phrase listed as 4.6. In the case mentioned, we will read the following: "Take care of walking where you should and make sure it is on a straight and safe path. You cannot be on both paths at the same time."

These parables and metaphors will combine to give the consultant and who seeks advice a final idea of the combination of the readings.

Number 1

1.1 = There are problems in and outside. May your mouth not bleed. Beware of the words you can say.

1.2 = If you shoot arrows, be careful not to hurt your family or your friends.

1.3 = Your enemies are still standing and they did not die. Take care of yourself, otherwise you will bleed.

1.4 = Sores and redness can appear on the entire body. Heal your body completely, on all sides and from one end to the other.

1.5 = Jealousy can destroy you, cement doubts and resentments that may affect you as well as others. There is revolution and disputes.

1.6 = Do not lose your head. Damn misfortune seeks a victim. Be careful and be reasonable. If you act like this with the truth on your side, you can execute all your steps. That way you will not lose or fail.

1.7 = Dreaming of the immensity of death will not affect you and if you dream of the sea, you will not drown. You do not have to be afraid of its depths.

1.8 = When you fear thieves, secure your home and protect yourself. In times of isolation, meditate on the dangers to take precautions for the future.

1.9 = Husband and wife who argue would bring misfortune to the house. They would open the door for those who want to steal their happiness.

1.10 = Avarice for the gold does not retain or increase its value. On the contrary, the gold dilutes and disappears from our hands. The one who grasps everything, very little of it or almost nothing will they have.

1.11 = Dishonesty and stubbornness bring harm and illness.

1.12 = A sea extinguishes a great fire because great problems are solved with great solutions. Do not try to minimize the problem because you will not solve it.

1.13 = Do not neglect your position or your mission. You have to be always alert and ready to comply. Otherwise, they would even kill you to snatch your belongings or try to get you sick.

1.14 = No one knows the beginning and the end of things.

1.15 = Discover the instigators and those who plan against you.

1.16 = All things have their negative and positive side. It's up to you to know how to use them.

Number 2

2.1 = See 1.2

2.2 = The unfaithful couple loses each other, but the woman who only lies expects the same fate.

2.3 = Avoid disputes and be careful of what you say. They will be aware of your words.

2.4 = There are many difficulties—do not try to suppress them all at once. Start with the smaller ones, being consistent, and you will see that you can counteract and finish with the others more easily.

2.5 = Money is not everything, but it avoids dislikes and tragedies. If you thank the Saints and fulfill what you promised, the good fortune will be with you.

2.6 = True change occurs when a being is transformed from the inside out. Everything else is ephemeral and superfluous.

2.7 = Do not talk too much because you will get tired. Do not eat too much because you will get sick. Do both things and your mouth will bleed.

2.8 = They want to dethrone the Obá by arrows, by force, and with violence.

2.9 = There are rumors between family and friends. Protect yourself from felonies and lies. There are problems at home and on the street.

2.10 = The one who gets up first takes more advantage of the day and treasures with more caution what he found early.

2.11 = Birds must fly to live; if imprisoned they will die.

2.12 = If you do not understand the language of the ancestors, you will not be able to hear the revelations of the snails and you will not be able to interpret the Odús.

2.13 = "Death to the King; Long live the King!"

2.14 = Not all losses are bad. Some are even necessary for renewal and constant living.

2.15 = No one can understand everything that has happened, is happening, or will happen.

2.16 = All things have to do with "the whole" because nothingness does not exist. "The whole" is anterior to nothing and every particle of it is in all things. You only have to find them to gather them and to be aware of "everything."

Number 3

3.1 = See 1.3

3.2 = See 2.3

3.3 = When you raise your voice and arrogantly argue, you do not hold the truth—you just try to impose yours.

3.4 = Where everything begins or ends. There are two different sides of the same coin where duality can get you in trouble with justice.

3.5 = Looking for what you abandoned or left behind, or just retired by choice, can bring misfortune. Ignore it, but do so with prudent and humble humility. Thank the Almighty in advance for consistency in acting.

3.6 = Measure yourself with what you want and don't abuse it, because you will lose more than you won. Don't keep what does not belong to you, or else in the future, someone will take it away.

3.7 = Why do you ask if you already know the answer? Revelation is within you.

3.8 = Do not destroy or go after what you, for some reason, have in your own home.

3.9 = It is best not to meddle in other people's affairs. The best thing to do is to secure your things and leave everything else in the hands of Providence.

3.10 = Forgive and forget—even if you are punished with violence. Whoever forgives is free from pain.

3.11 = You are not responsible for others' karma; everyone must solve their own affairs. You can only help, but without assuming responsibility for others.

3.12 = The heart and the brain make things fair and just. If any fail, the imbalance brings defeat and failure.

3.13 = Water cannot be drunk with dirty hands because what you drink would make you sick.

3.14 = No matter what kind of instrument was used to hurt you, whatever it was, you would bleed from the wound.

3.15 = You have to know how to drink so you do not harm your body, and you have to shut your mouth when you should not drink more. Recognize your limits and that of the person who offers you another drink.

3.16 = People often pay very dearly for the will of a few.

Number 4

4.1 = See 1.4

4.2 = See 2.4

4.3 = See 3.4

4.4 = If you do not take care of your things, no one will do it for you. If you received them, you must preserve them or you will lose them. You must also protect your people because you can only safeguard them.

4.5 = Be careful with the spirit of the dead who roams without stopping and will not stop until they find someone. Run and hide, take the necessary precautions to avoid misfortune. Nothing will fructify unless you take the necessary measures.

4.6 = Beware of walking where you should and make sure it is a straight and safe path. You cannot be on both paths at the same time.

4.7 = If the head does not direct the body, the body will not walk well and your steps will be foolish. Think, otherwise no one will be interested in you because of your great incongruity.

4.8 = If you were born to be the first, you cannot be the last. It is not right to contradict what is planned. Do not fool yourself.

4.9 = To walk safely is to look where you walk without neglecting the rear and at the same time without distracting yourself with what lies ahead. You cannot retrace your path, because your footprints will remain there even if you want to hide them.

4.10 = The presumed receives little credit.

4.11 = If you are not clean and pure enough, do not meddle with sacred things, because you will end up being defiled and you will have great shame.

4.12 = Do not rush. Sometimes those who take their time come before and do their job.

4.13 = To have children is a mission, and worrying about them will be your responsibility.

4.14 = A birth and a fight culminate in a hospital.

4.15 = You cannot teach a seaman anything. The fisherman can guide you in the great mysteries.

4.16 = Get rid of possessions and look forward to your prize.

Number 5

5.1 = See 1.5

5.2 = See 2.5

5.3 = See 3.5

5.4 = See 4.5

5.5 = You must act and proceed quickly. There could be a mess and chaos in everything. The best advice is to talk less and act more.

5.6 = It is easy to appreciate everything outdoors. That is when you are free of walls and oppressions and you can distinguish between two ways of thinking and find a balance. Progress is out in the open.

5.7 = Even if you are free of charges and suspicion, do not boast about it because good fortune will not always be on your side. There was no evidence against you but bragging would be dangerous. Be careful what you speak, and if you owe something, keep your word.

5.8 = Not to act with lies is to act with intelligence. Omitting or hiding is also a lie, and whether you like it or not, it is always discovered. Nothing escapes the eyes of God. You could lose your most valuable thing (love) by lying. Be careful. Keep your promises by telling the truth and value the things you have now.

5.9 = Take care of your loved ones and the things with which God blesses you. Appreciate and love them now that you have them. Tomorrow may be too late. Do it today and you will get rewards, otherwise you will have negative karma. Take care of your things and keep your word.

5.10 = You must hide neither misfortune nor good fortune, nor sadness or joy. It is better to act honestly to avoid what you don't want. Act and work truly according to what you live by. Seek spiritual help. That is the answer.

5.11 = Playing with fire is dangerous because you could burn.

5.12 = What you don't learn in this world, you will learn it in the hereafter.

5.13 = There are open depths. Take precautions because there you will find activity and not passivity.

5.14 = Good fortune may be within your reach, but certain obstacles prevent it from reaching you with its royal splendor.

5.15 = You must honor your debts, duties, and all your promises and you will rest in peace.

5.16 = There will be no modifications that are more negative compared to what is happening. Maybe changing your strategy or place is not the solution to your problems.

Number 6

6.1 = See 1.6

6.2 = See 2.6

6.3 = See 3.6

6.4 = See 4.6

6.5 = See 5.6

6.6 = A true King never dies in the memory of his people, for he who rules with intelligence and equity is a wise man who time cannot destroy.

6.7 = You can only walk in a single direction in a single moment. Do not miss being in two places at once because it's impossible. In spite of having four cardinal points, you'll not be able to walk in four directions at the same time. A heart cannot beat love for two people at once because one of them will be deceived. Or worst of all, in the end, the deceived is you.

6.8 = Respect for the ancestral brings you experience. Time is wise and knows when something begins and must culminate. Everything is at its exact point and measure. Acting without hustle or in a hurry will give you the opportunity to meditate and analyze things.

6.9 = Do not talk senseless and do not lie, otherwise you will be considered fanciful or a liar and people will not believe in you. You will become a victim of your own lies and follies. You must know to value each thing and don't mystify.

6.10 = A true King cannot contradict himself or have a double opinion. Foolishness and incongruity cannot govern a people well. You must change your attitude and observe consistent behavior. There cannot be two commands at the same time.

6.11 = Pretending, lying, or envying are grave faults. Pretending what is not could cause what is not desired and cause you to be a slave to what is wanted or pretended in raving enslavement.

6.12 = Stubbornness brings defeat. You must rule alone and things will change.

6.13 = Those who are accustomed to lying and falsifying have two hearts and double faces.

6.14 = If you reject what you must accept, sooner or later your duty quota will increase.

6.15 = Those who behave with the truth are fortunate and those who lie are unhappy.

6.16 = Every sovereign is inherited by a successor.

Number 7

7.1 = See 1.7

7.2 = See 2.7

7.3 = See 3.7

7.4 = See 4.7

7.5 = See 5.7

7.6 = See 6.7

7.7 = Those who work for their parents do good things and are good children. Who is a good son is a good father and husband. Be faithful to your wife and you will be loyal to your family.

7.8 = Forgetting or despising your own traditions is foolish. Think about it and you will see that what you learned from childhood and your elders are wise things. If you change this scale of values, there will be uneasiness. If you respect your parents, you will be touched by the grace of God.

7.9 = Do not waste on futile and unnecessary things. Not everything that is presented to you is appealing or good to consume.

7.10 = To be an honest person is to obey and fulfill the mandates.

7.11 = Do not waste on futile and unnecessary things. Not everything that is presented to you is appealing or good for you.

7.12 = Wait for the final results to see how things turn out. Be patient.

7.13 = Who knows how to reason knows how to wait and listen carefully.

7.14 = If both have a big nose, it will be difficult to kiss.

7.15 = If you want to shoot drifting, try to have a firm and secure base. Are you actually doing the right thing? Confirm the mechanisms, your steps, and your action.

7.16 = Find out what the source was and how all things started.

Number 8

8.1 = See 1.8

8.2 = See 2.8

8.3 = See 3.8

8.4 = See 4.8

8.5 = See 5.8

8.6 = See 6.8

8.7 = See 7.8

8.8 = No matter how hard and painful a wound is, it always ends up healing. The pain and the complaint cease, the days of misfortune pass. Likewise, take care of your loved ones, especially your friends, because otherwise you could stay away from them.

8.9 = If you wait for the correct moment, you could see the results. It's not worth rushing. The eagerness brings poor results and is typical of a person with little experience. Don't repeat mistakes, otherwise it will only bring you back delays and difficulties by keeping you away from your goals.

8.10 = It is not advisable to owe something to someone important and restless. You will not be able to enjoy anything since your creditor, being witty and very active, will not cease until you comply with what is owed and promised. In these cases, it is good to have the help of your family or those you consider like family, even without blood ties.

8.11 = Underestimation is wrong, but the overvaluation is even worse. If you want to ascend in your life, humility should be your ally. Pride is the best vehicle to fall into disaster. The door of the true abyss is called egocentrism. Try to have high esteem without falling into excesses, because the balance of values is necessary to create the right foundations. Recognize yourself for what you are, your real value, what you support or represent. This is the first step you must take to ascending the path of life.

8.12 = Who has been unjustly disadvantaged will rise. Who has gained power by taking advantage of others will succumb and fail. Then, there will be calm and everyone will get what deserved. The darkness of confusion will disappear to give way to light.

8.13 = Whoever consumes unhealthy things will not feel pleasure, and his blood, his soul, and his body will become sick. It will sprout from his flesh and his skin will fester. True pleasure is in things that bring benefit to the body and evolution to the human psyche and soul.

8.14 = The wise and prudent is the one who knows how to differentiate the singing of the birds from the villages and from the jungles. Although they look the same, they are different birds with different songs. Each has a different habitat.

8.15 = Strong measures would put an end to serious problems. For big problems, big solutions. Solve problems quickly so they won't transcend in time. The cold turns off the heat. Heat, as a dynamic force, will also strive for balance. In the compensation obtained from the two forces, we'll find the balance.

8.16 = You should not stop; on the contrary, you must continue. Everything will come in moderation and in due course. No fuss or being out of control. Wisdom is not obtained from one day to another. There we find the determined processes, the established time, and the continuity in the action. These factors are necessary to establishing the knowledge that will reach the true wisdom of the soul.

Number 9

9.1 = See 1.9

9.2 = See 2.9

9.3 = See 3.9

9.4 = See 4.9

9.5 = See 5.9

9.6 = See 6.9

9.7 = See 7.9

9.8 = See 8.9

9.9 = If from the beginning things were like this, you can no longer change the principles, and it is better to leave things as they started. Be wary of a bad friend because he can betray you. The false friend appears in sheepskin, but behind that facade hides a wild animal about to attack. However, vertiginous changes halfway are not advisable because they would bring more harm than good. Take the necessary precautions to avoid getting hurt; stay away and measure the possibilities to get ahead in these proceedings.

9.10 = You do not want to see reality and yet will be present. Some time will pass but reality will come before your eyes. Truth and reality are hidden just as your enemies are. The curtain that covers them will open and you will see everything. This time you will be almost like a spectator. Do not deny what your eyes see or ignore what your ears hear.

9.11 = In a contest there is no room for two victors or a laurel crown that could be shared. The only way to do that would be to undo the crown. If so, there would be nothing to crown the winner. Show to win, rise to the occasion with dignity and nobility, and victory will be yours.

9.12 = Pay attention to all your things so they do not fail. Take all necessary precautions so that nothing is adrift. Clutter can lead to defeat.

9.13 = What has been said nobody can deny. What is done, it is done. Meditate before giving judgment or giving an opinion. Study carefully what is presented before channeling an action or materialize some effort that could create some future action.

9.14 = There must be no death or betrayal between friends. If you betray a true friend, you will kill him in life. There will be no forgiveness. Slowly and without realizing it, you would kill the possibility of having frank and dignified people at your side. If so, solitude will be your end inexorably.

9.15 = To incite the death of others is to invite death into your own abode. If you associate with death, you will not be able to separate it from your life. Be careful! Its influence is powerful and arrives unannounced, opens all doors without prejudices of social or cultural classes. It covers all peoples, races, and continents. When death arrives, we can hear its steps, we can feel it even if we cannot see it. You must not have death as an enemy or an ally.

9.16 = The rain is a blessing of all Saints and Olodumaré. She heals all wounds (even those that are not seen), purifies all things, washes our auric field, clears the mind, and sweeps away impurities. This element is present in the interpretation of this combination to help and support who is consulting. These forces will unlock your way and clean things that are not vibrating in its frequency.

Number 10

10.1 = See 1.10

10.2 = See 2.10

10.3 = See 3.10

10.4 = See 4.10

10.5 = See 5.10

10.6 = See 6.10

10.7 = See 7.10

10.8 = See 8.10

10.9 = See 9.10

10.10 = Whenever you are looking for, you will find a solution. Analyze all the details and do not leave anything without taking account. Even the smallest clues will help you find the answer you need. The union of feelings creates strength. Turn to your loved ones and seek the advice and experience of your elders. Everyone can remember and provide data and memories to reach a solution.

10.11 = The practical should not alter the feelings and the unconcern should not fall into indolence. Idleness and lack of practicality are not attributes of a rational mind. A heart can be practical without being materialistic. It may be impractical and not lose coherence. You can also be carefree without becoming indolent. Only the rational can handle these precepts and maintain the unalterable principles of judgments.

10.12 = You're the sole owner of your paths and your life. Organize your course and your steps will be calm and safe and your life will be calm and clear. You are the only one who walks your path. Even your own shadow cannot emulate you because cannot walk unless you decide to.

10.13 = "Do good to all" and the balance of karmic rewards will benefit you when eternal wisdom deems it necessary for your evolution. Intelligent beings work with the forces of good. Ignorant beings act with dark or misguided forces. The good protects and rewards you; evil forces forsake and punish you. Do not forget that only you are the one who is rewarded or punished, because it's up to you which path you walk.

10.14 = Always teach as an example of what you have learned and what you put into practice. It must be a true morality and not a simple oratory or words in vain. Don't proclaim what you don't do or cannot fulfill due to lack of will, ability, or desire. You must be the reflection of what you think, the materialization of what you express, and the action of what you promise.

10.15 = You cannot hide or deny your shadow, or even reject it as long as there is light. You will have to face the truth in spite of the fears and insecurities. Fears only create false images that contradict reality. The reality is there and you cannot hide it in the same way that you cannot hide the sun with a finger. Even if you close your eyes, you cannot make it disappear. It will only disappear from your vision, but it will still be there.

10.16 = Behave with justice, but do not apply it with your hand— leave that to the Almighty. Only he knows human destinies. The ways of God's justice are untiring to the human mind capacity. Just try to be fair, equitable, and above all things, always have mercy and pity.

Number 11

11.1 = See 1.11

11.2 = See 2.11

11.3 = See 3.11

11.4 = See 4.11

11.5 = See 5.11

11.6 = See 6.11

11.7 = See 7.11

11.8 = See 8.11

11.9 = See 9.11

11.10 = See 10.11

11.11 = Being alone does not mean that you really are. Learn to listen to the sound of silence, and you will know that beyond you, there is a world where fury and placidness coexist, the dualities of deafening silences and calming noises. When you truly understand the solitary unity of the one, the two will arrive, and this will multiply, successively creating the majority. Then, it will be a matter of choosing where you stand and where you want to be. Begin your inner journey that will lead you first to yourself and then make you meet all and all things. The key is to meet again.

11.12 = As a human being, you are composed of the flesh and the Divine. You will never be at all good or at all bad, nor will you be completely true or totally wrong. When you think otherwise, you will have begun to be. It is as simple as the night before the day. Remember: "At the beginning, everything was darkness."

11.13 = Not always will the fight and the discussion lead you to victory. Sometimes the ecstasy and the placidness of the quiet wait along with resignation, which in no way is a waiver, can lead you to success. Victory and success do not always spread or make deafening noises in their wake. Many times you will not hear the fanfares of the trumpets winning on earth, but in the hereafter there will be a chorus of souls singing your victory when it is just and valid.

11.14 = You should not respond in an offensive way to hurtful questions. To respond intelligently is to do it with truth but without hurting, with prudence but without weakness. Thus there will be no violence but tranquility.

11.15 = Whoever does not know how to smile won't have his heart open. You won't have the capacity to create a family or expand your seed. Whoever does not know how to extend his hand can hardly attract his company in life. To open oneself to others often has its implicit risk, but closure also has its negative side; it brings pain to the spirit and solitude to the soul and matter.

11.16 = Not the most powerful, rich, strong, or captivating in the world is more important, powerful, rich, strong, or captivating than the beauty of the spirit. This condition makes you free and you can be happy.

Number 12

12.1 = See 1.12

12.2 = See 2.12

12.3 = See 3.12

12.4 = See 4.12

12.5 = See 5.12

12.6 = See 6.12

12.7 = See 7.12

12.8 = See 8.12

12.9 = See 9.12

12.10 = See 10.12

12.11 = See 11.12

12.12 = If you want to win in the contest, be calm, orderly, judicious, alert, and attentive to the movements. Carelessness can be fatal and determining. Do not show up rampaging or raucous. Do not boast about victory until the last word is said, and yet don't presume. While you're celebrating, others could rejoice vilely against you. Time is everything, and among the things it expresses, is the victory of those who conquered with nobility and dignity.

12.13 = All the herbs on earth will not cure you unless you look inside, and in an act of humility, you give yourself to the needy to help in his suffering. Only then can you overcome the pain, the sorrows, the sadness, and the uncertainty.

12.14 = All the things that don't work for your family, don't work for you either. There are no solitary joys or unrecognized rewards. A true celebration is the one that is shared with those who really take pride and joy in our triumphs.

12.15 = Treat others as you would like to be treated, otherwise disease and misfortune will knock on your door. What you throw, you will receive. That is the law of compensation. If you were hurt, let your wound heal. Only time and love would cure.

12.16 = What stagnates does not vibrate. If it does not vibrate, it is not in a cycle of evolution. Reject and accept what vibrates at a high frequency because it is the only way to transcend to other, higher planes.

Number 13

13.1 = See 1.13

13.2 = See 2.13

13.3 = See 3.13

13.4 = See 4.13

13.5 = See 5.13

13.6 = See 6.13

13.7 = See 7.13

13.8 = See 8.13

13.9 = See 9.13

13.10 = See 10.13

13.11 = See 11.13

13.12 = See 12.13

13.13 = Introspection and ostracism is wrong. Looking for examples is not, but if you keep searching, you will not reach conclusions and you will drown in questions. If you are not careful, you could become your own victim. Open yourself, leave the confinement, and you will see everything different.

13.14 = Success and defeat can touch each other at an imperceptible point. They can be together when they are ephemeral in their existence, or represent both sides of the same coin. It is important to know how to differentiate and separate them in time so that, despite being different at the beginning, they do not get confused, or worse, join completely.

13.15 = If you want to know if people cry and do not forget about you, you could lie and disguise yourself by personifying your death in your own funeral. Would you take that risk for so little? Think how necessary it is for you to know it. Remember, true emotions and feelings are often internal and invisible to the eyes that cannot perceive them.

13.16 = Stop proclaiming the defects of others. Instead, look for your own mistakes to better understand others and be able to modify your own shortcomings. Highlighting others' mistakes will make them reluctant to confess their misunderstandings and they will retreat. It will make them insecure to such an extent that their mistakes will become more frequent and deeper, finally creating a gulf of pain on both sides that will be very difficult to correct.

Number 14

14.1 = See 1.14

14.2 = See 2.14

14.3 = See 3.14

14.4 = See 4.14

14.5 = See 5.14

14.6 = See 6.14

14.7 = See 7.14

14.8 = See 8.14

14.9 = See 9.14

14.10 = See 10.14

14.11 = See 11.14

14.12 = See 12.14

14.13 = See 13.14

14.14 = There is the right time to react and act regardless of the outcome. If you chose the time and the opportunity well, the
result will be satisfactory.

14.15 = The reprimand of a wise man is more beneficial than the praise
of an ignorant one or the adulation of a fool. The reprimand
will make you progress. The wisdom with which you are cor-
rected shows the nobility of who corrects you. Nobility is a
condition of the true wise. The flattery of a fool will increase
your error and ignorance.

14.16 = You don't have centuries to live and you are only aware of one
life (the one you are living in right now). Do not be indolent;
do things now because time goes by and you do not wait. There
is a biological clock and another of eternal time. The needles
of both revolve in the endless wheel of life to which no one
can escape. Live well every minute of your life!

Number 15

15.1 = See 1.15

15.2 = See 2.15

15.3 = See 3.15

15.4 = See 4.15

15.5 = See 5.15

15.6 = See 6.15

15.7 = See 7.15

15.8 = See 8.15

15.9 = See 9.15

15.10 = See 10.15

15.11 = See 11.15

15.12 = See 12.15

15.13 = See 13.15

15.14 = See 14.15

15.15 = Use what you need for your life without abusing anything, because use and not abuse is the key to everything. Otherwise, the source of life perishes in this plane. Excessive use is abuse and abusing leads to destruction.

15.16 = If you have rejected something, it's because you had your reasons and you don't have to regret it. What falls can be lifted itself, even when it is something inanimate.

Number 16

16.1 = See 1.16

16.2 = See 2.16

16.3 = See 3.16

16.4 = See 4.16

16.5 = See 5.16

16.6 = See 6.16

16.7 = See 7.16

16.8 = See 8.16

16.9 = See 9.16

16.10 = See 10.16

16.11 = See 11.16

16.12 = See 12.16

16.13 = See 13.16

16.14 = See 14.16

16.15 = See 15.16

16.16 = You have the prophetic gift of divination. You have the kingdom and the people, but it is necessary to crown the King
and establish the just and noble monarch. Find the answers
within a true Obá and you will see that the answer is yourself. Maybe you should take many turns in your life to finally
realize that everything was there close, very close. It does not
matter. Everything you had to walk through was the experience that was accumulating so that light and life could shine
more in your way.

8: Opelé: Divination with the Chain of Ifá

Oracles of Ifá

The Opelé, or chain of Ifá, is an indispensable divinatory element of the fortune-teller. It is formed by two lines or two "hands" consisting of eight parts of the palm nuts, representing Ifá or Orumilá (also known as Urumilá and Orunmilá.)

A legend tells that Orungá, son of Aganjú and Yemayá, was the one who planted the first palm tree, from which the nuts were extracted to form the first Rosary of Ifá. The name of Orungá is known and sometimes invoked as *moyubando* (a type of recitation as an invocation) by the parents of the secret, the foreseers or Babalawos.

The fruits of the palm are called Ikines and have a sacred connotation because they represent the sixteen eyes of Ifá in the number of primary combinations of the Odús. From the same tree, an oil or butter is obtained that is used in the creation of meals, offerings, ebós, rituals, etc. In Africa it is known under different names: *Abobe, De-Kla, De-Yayá, Di-Bopé,*

Ade-Koi, Adersan, Dendém, and others. In Cuba it is known as *manteca de corojo,* and in Brazil the extracted oily product is known as dendé oil.

These fruits are extracted from the palm tree. The tree has sacred characteristics and serves as a material home for Ifá to create the magical contact between men and the gods, establishing the designs of the future. When we speak of Ifá, we must be clear that we are referring to the system of divination used by the Babalawo in their predictions and interpretations.

We are talking about the 4096 Odús, the result of the 256 from the multiplication and integration of the sixteen main Odús, among themselves. Orumilá, son of Oduduwa and Yembo, owns all of the Oracles and all of the ceremonial rites of Ifá. He was the last Orishá to be born and his power came last to Earth. This is the reason why he knows all the secrets and all that happened to each of the Orishás, since his energy already presided in a latent state of action in the Cosmos. He knows and understands the present, the past, and the future of every person before they incarnate and after their death.

In readings with the Opelé, each Odú is presented with a specific roll from the chain or rosary of the Orishá of divination, and the reading is based on the different convex or concave positions that result from the palm nuts. There can be sixteen interpretations, always taking into account the way the rosary falls and marking one right side and one left side for reading and interpreting. These are archetypes (*Olodú*).

When handling the sixteen Ikines (the hardest part of the fruit or seed of the palm tree), respect for Babalawo becomes something ancestrally magical and very powerful. A union of the sixteen eyes of Orumilá and the sixteen windows of the palace of Obatalá begins to take place. The priest tries to grab everyone with his left hand (an intuitive way to use our right brain lobe) at once and then begins the invocations concerned.

In this way he is ready to mark on the Opon Ifá (the Ifá divination board). If one Ikine is left out of the game on the first verification, he will make two marks in the right zone. If there are two Ikines remaining in the second verification, it will be marked on the left side of Opon Ifá.

Odd is equivalent to two marks and even is equivalent to one mark. Depending on the order of the rolls, the left or right zone marks the binary style of demarcation by which the Ifá system acts and is represented by at the same time. This is based on a double grouping in two columns that result from four linear figures when they are Meji (doubles) (see appendix for the representations of the Meji).

All known Odú combinations belong to the Dafa group. Each Ikine is not only the means by which we can come into contact with what we would call Ile Awo (earth, place, house, or in a more generalized aspect, the worldview of divination or the territory of secrecy). It also represents the living symbol of the perpetual generation of life as the seed and source of hope for the regeneration of every living being. In that perfect cycle, life and death are linked in a single aspect that is the eternity of the cycles that never end, which bring the messages and the wisdom of the times.

The representation of the Dafa system is made up of two vertical lines. One line is considered the first step to open and develop the channel of the primary or masculine element in the symbolic sense of life. Double lines symbolize the unity and concentration of efforts to preserve life, to foster it with a regenerative aspect, symbolizing the female element.

Both symbolize answer and question, expansion and concentration, the abstract and the concrete. Both are the perfect sides of a sphere submitted to a whole. From the game of the single and double lines, we reach the 256 octagrams. They are the result of the combination of the sixteen main Odús with their ramifications. They relate myths and legends intertwined with each other rich in examples and actively interrelated.

Each one is titled with old African metaphorical phrases that I have tried to assimilate and adapt to facilitate their understanding to the reader, inserting them in the world in which we live. It is also in the religious practice of believers that is effective in the field of prophecy. Adapting the metaphorical phrases became necessary for a better understanding of the modern man without losing validity or ethnic and cultural values. This was done in addition to respecting symbols and roots that I consider unalterable and imperturbable.

The Oracles of Ifá are not just simple oracles. On the contrary, they are all the wisdom and experience of ancestral power. It reveals the ethical and moral values by which any human group that values themselves as part of a civilization should take into account.

Like the Ten Commandments, or the wisdom teachings, they exercised and still exercise rules of conduct and procedures to continue to differentiate Good from Evil by creating guidelines and rules of coexistence for human beings.

The myths and legends are fused not in an illusory, utopian, unrealizable way but in an entirely palpable and sobering way. In short, all divinatory techniques come together at an indeterminate point, unthinkable or indecipherable to the human mind, governed by divine desires. But those who put into practice some of them are synchronized in time and distance in a way that is incomprehensible for those who reason with rigid and narrow parameters. Therefore, the mind of the soothsayer must travel, transcend his own body, and fly like birds (symbols of Ifá) so that from the heavens his ears hear what others cannot hear and his eyes see what the retina of no other human being can see.

This magical journey is made by the Babalawo (who knows the mysteries), by the Orishá-Awo (the one used of Merindiloggún), or by any Shaman.

Configuration of Each Roll in Ifá
Odús of Ifá

Of the sixteen Odús of Ifá, the numbers 1, 2, 4, and 7 are considered major or principal. Coincidentally, the sum of these numbers results in the number 14, which is the mathematical representation of two seven sums. (Remember the importance within magic and esotericism of the number 7 as magic par excellence.) If we reduce the 14 to a number of a single unit (1+4), this gives us the number 5, which is the representation of balance in someone who uses its potentialities logically.

The symbols of the demarcations belonging to the Major Odús would represent the conception of the fundamentals of Ifá. These are Eyiogbe Meji, Oyekún Meji, Obara Meji, and Odí Meji.

Configurations

Obara Meji: Sector right and left (each one with an individual roll with the convex side, and the subsequent three with the concave side.)

Okana Meji: Inverse in the arrangement with respect to the roll of the previous one.

Oyekún Meji: When on both sides (right and left), they roll on each part, with the four halves on the concave side.

Ogundá Meji: The right and left sector with three rolls, each with the convex side, but the last with the concave side.

Osá Meji: Inverse to the previous roll.

Iroso Meji: The right and left sector with two rolls in a row with the convex side, and the last two rolls with the concave side.

Ojuaní Meji: Inverse to the previous roll.

Oché Meji: The first and third roll in the right and left sectors with convex sides, the second and fourth roll with concave side.

Ofún Meji: Inverse to the previous roll.

Iwori Meji: When on both sides, right and left, they roll once with the halves on the concave side, then twice on the convex side, and at the end once with the concave side.

Odí Meji: Inverse to the previous roll.

Eyiogbe Meji: When on both sides, right and left, they roll with the four halves with the convex side.

Iká Meji: The first roll in the right and left sector have the concave side, the second roll has the convex side and the last two with the concave sides.

Otrupo Meji: Inverse to the previous roll.

Otura Meji: The first, third, and fourth rolls in the right and left sectors have the convex side. The second roll have the concave side.

Ireté Meji: Inverse to the previous roll.

Invocation Before Beginning to Register

Ago Ifá: Permission Ifá

Ago Ile Awo Yin Emu: License land of the soothsayer, Permission of the Oracle, talk to me

Ifá She Eti Uyi Ogbon Emi: Ifá give me worthy and wise ears

She Ade Oba La Emi: Give me the crown of King

Ifá L'Annu: You are merciful

Awo She Oro Mi: Divine teacher, give me prosperity

Fun Mi Ni Iré: Bring me good fortune

Awo La Yana Wa Dahunnmi: High Diviner, please respond to me

Odukue Ola Ifá: Thank you Ifá.

Steps That the Fortune-Teller Follows

After playing with the Opelé, the Ilé destined for such purposes begins to *moyubar* by first saluting the top, then placing it in the third place on the right, and then on the left. Then they invoke Eshú to be an intermediary between the real world and the spiritual world. Then they invoke Ifá and ask for his intercession in order to cross the *Orita Meta* (the invisible line that separates both spheres). Then they invoke the *Orún* (The Other World) so that the eternal may be present by saying:

Olodumaré Nzame

Babá Nkwa Olofi

Ol0dumare Dara Dun

Olodumaré Dara Mada

Dara Ogbón

Olorun, Eleda

Odumare, Eleemi

Oro Oro Oro

Orumilá

Agó

Thus their mind transcends the boundaries of the eternal by mentioning the name of God, the Father and Creator, from whom it is impossible to imagine all its splendor and magnificence, trying to descend from Him the light of knowledge to link the connection with Orumilá. Then they end up saying "Agó" (asking for permission or license) to enter the world of prophecy.

After finishing the previous prayer, he continues with others and immediately invokes the ancestors, the great diviners he has known and ends with the name of those who have trained him as a priest, including the names of his godparents.

The Word and the Voice of Orumilá

The maxims of Orumilá arrive by means of their use by the fortune-teller of the chain that receives the name seen previously (Opelé or Okpelé de Ifá). The maxims could have eight parts of kola nuts, or can be joined by a chain of metal links. Necklaces or rosaries are also often found joining the nuts by several braided rows of African straw (a very similar material to raffia of great consistency and durability).

Both points of the Opelé represent the stages of human life (cycles that are never interrupted) based on the belief of eternity or the immortality of the soul. One end symbolizes the masculine principle of creation (or its active part), and the other the feminine that ends in several strips or threads of the same material. When rolled and consulting with the Opelé, it must fall in the form of a U (the open part is placed facing the priest), the male part on the right side and the female on the left.

In different areas of Africa, where the Yoruba culture transcended its own lands, there is a variation of this rosary called Abiggbá. Here, respecting the configuration of the number sixteen, four nuts are used in each one of the four chains that comprise this system. Here we take into account a representation considered more sidereal and used in reference to the four cardinal points and the four stations that represent life on the planet. Before starting the divination, we greet both the ancestors and the cardinal points, North, South, West, and East, in this order.

Bearing in mind that in each of the directions dwells and lives a specific force. When invoking it from the center the fortune-teller, represented in the Abiggbá by means of the fusion of the chains, it will bring knowledge related to every living thing that inhabits those zones, no matter how distant they may be. Symbolically there are representations of the four elements of nature: earth, water, air, and fire. These elements are essential for the fortune-teller to be in accordance with life and thus be able to fulfill his mission.

We see the repetition of the number four and its combinations in the system of divination and consultation based perhaps on the Yoruba belief of the four main days in the week. The first of the days, the *Ojhó Awo* (day of the fortune-teller), is dedicated to or ruled by Orumilá, the *Ojhó Ogún* is ruled by Ogún, the *Ojhó Acutá* (the day of the owner of the stones) is governed by Shangó, and finally the *Ojhó Obatalá* is dedicated to the Orishá of the same name, also known as Oxalá or Orixalá.

The relation is also seen in some nations or lineages of worship within Santería that attribute an energy or ruling force to each cardinal point: the North for Ogún, the South for Orixalá, the West for Shangó, and the East for Eshú, the messenger of Ifá.

9: Other Tools and Methods in African Divination

The History of the Eight Most Powerful Plants

In the beginning of life on this planet, Olodumaré (the creator of all things) established the supremacy of eight very powerful plants in the vegetable kingdom. The function of these plants was to act together and in synchronization to help the development of evolution. Despite this premise, seeing themselves more influential and stronger than others, they began to feel jealousy, envy, and vanity among themselves. In their attempt to surpass their own power, they forgot their mutual dependence that was necessary to survive, since that and no other had been the objective of the establishment of their power.

Among the eight plants there were four that were the oldest and the most advanced. They defined the planes of life and acting systematically with their other four sisters played a free game of compensation without equivocation. In a balanced way, the game put into action all the necessary and indispensable steps in the endless wheel of the indefectible cycles of life.

These four were the most important ones:

Iré: the good

Ikú: death or transmutation of life in different planes

Anó: the disease

Eyó: the tragic dispute

And, the first four were followed in order of importance by the four minors:

Ofó: the sudden losses

Ona: the strong falls, metaphorically speaking, directly in the epidermis, in the skin, animals' sufferings, material or spiritual difficulties

Acobá: the sudden and unexpected

Fitibo: the news, the new, and could represent in its most negative face, the news of a sudden death

Even between the two plants in superior positions, which due to their condition were hierarchically distanced from the next two of the first group, there was tremendous jealousy. Despite being in a good position, and without the need to prove their superiority between the two, rivalry was also beginning to appear.

When something had to die (moving to another state of vibration and life), Iré did not respect Ikú's decision and got in his way, trying to show that he could change his plans, and making it difficult many times for Anó to replenish and fortify whoever was weak and/or sick. Many times the situations were reversed.

The result was always the same: chaos and total disorder. This presented a delay in the steps that, without mediating the individual karma of each being and things, had to be carried out as a synchronized balance in the wheel of life.

To correct the erroneous behavior, Olofi, the ruler of the earth, ordered each of the main plants to do ebó to establish again the order between them and the priorities in the scale of mandates necessary for the infinite circle of evolution to turn without detours or setbacks.

He told the first four plants that everything in life had an order of priorities and a location in that order. That order should be respected to achieve the degrees of harmony and that peace would only be possible by respecting those steps.

And then he advised the other four plants that as in the beginning, they should obey their elders. Iré, considering that everything good belonged to her, decided not to do her part of the ebó. This is the reason why, from that moment on, it is considered that good things don't last forever, or at least, they're not permanent.

Eyó was the first to fulfill the mandate of Olofi, and as a prize he preserved his place. Ikú also fulfilled the mandate and as a reward he obtained that always, at some point in the life of the planet, he would play an important role and would be present. Nothing would be eternal or good forever because of the lack of Iré, who would not always be present and could be discarded.

However, sooner or later Ikú would be present without making distinctions whatsoever. Anó could appear, suddenly working with Fitibó, to obtain permission from his elders. From then on, the four minors were seconded the actions of the first ones and were used to solve or try to fix the problems of beings.

The Different Paths

Reconsidering about this story of the eight most powerful plants and about the need to have an absolute order of respect and perfect synchronism gives us the idea of the possibilities that we can have a letter represented by the Iré or the Osobbos, and it is necessary to know the reasons why they come.

It is very important to know the Iré. In doing so, even the meaning of a negative letter can vary when a perfect Iré or Moyare is achieved. On the other hand, when all or some of the questions are negative, the good that it brings is imperfect (an Iré Coto-Yare) and it is something that is beneficial but incomplete.

List of the Iré

Iré Ari-Ikú: the good comes from the side of the spirits of the dead.

Iré Otonogwá: the good comes by means of all the sky and all its court.

Iré Elese-Orishá: the good comes specifically from a certain Orishá, or from some of them related to your spiritual capacity.

Iré Iya-Agba: the good comes from a grandmother.

Iré Baba-Agba: the good comes from a grandfather.

Iré Elese Orí-lnu: the good comes from your own conscience.

Iré Emí: the good is due to your spirit.

Iré Elese Eleda: the good comes from your own Guardian Angel.

Iré Omo: the good comes from a son.

Iré Oko: the good comes from a husband.

Iré Okuní: the good comes from a man.

Iré Aye: the good comes from things of this world.

Iré Orún: the good comes from the other world.

Iré Ara-Orún: the good comes from the side of the ancestors.

Iré Elese Egun: the good comes from a spirit of a dead person who knew you.

Iré Babá: the good comes from a father.

Iré Ogbiní: the good comes from a woman.

Iré Iyá: the good comes from a mother.

Iré Iyawo: the good comes from a wife.

Iré Ologberi: the good comes to you through unknown people, or from other places, from foreigners or strangers.

Iré Owó: the good comes through money.

Iré Aya: the good comes from the wife.

Iré Babá-Oko: the good comes from the father-in-law.

Iré Iyako: the good comes from the mother-in-law.

Iré Egbon: the good comes from the older brother or sister of the family.

List of the Osobbos

The established order is the one mentioned in the story that talks about the origin of Iré and the Osobbos: Ikú, Anó, Eyó, Ofó, Ona, Acaba, and Fitibó.

The Santero will try to ensure that these Osobbos do not become present either in the reading or in the life of the consultant. For that, and after moyubar (salute), he will say the following:

—*Kosi Ikú:* let there be no death.

Many times it is considered necessary to specify and clarify where death could come or the causes that could cause it as a protective measure to leave no path open to Ikú and in this way magically remove all possibilities through the power of the verb and prayer. Then it is said:

—*Kosi Ikú Ainá:* that there is no death by fire.

—*Kosi Ikú Loghí:* that there is no death by tomb.

—*Kosi Ikú Ara Ayé:* that there is no death by curses.

—*Kosi Ikú Akuse:* that there is no death by poverty.

—*Kosi Ikú Ika:* there is no death by witchcraft.

—*Kosi Ikú Ija:* that there is no death due to fights

And then keep saying:

—*Kosi Anó:* that there is no disease.

—*Kosi Eyó:* that there are no disputes or tragedies.

—*Kosi Ofó:* that there are no losses of loved ones.

—*Kosi Oná:* that there are no setbacks, spiritual problems, or issues with guardian angels, or misfortunes in material life (since the meaning of the obstacles in this case is quite great).

—*Kosi Acobá:* that there is no evil, that in no way cannot be prevented, or the unexpected not calculated.

It ends by saying:

—*Aikú Babagwa:* may good and eternal things come.

It begins by registering two letters even if the first one that appears belongs to a greater Odú. The ibó is delivered as it's described above. Then the hand is requested, asking if it brings Iré or Osobbo.

The first thing to know if it brings Iré is to check if it has a good path (Ebboda) or if the good is for the consultant. After the first two throws, and before specifying the third one, the Santero places the ibó. If a greater Odú came out here, the Santero would ask for the left hand. If the efún in this found in that hand, the answer is Iré. It constitutes an Iré Ari-Ikú. Then, questions are asked and the answers will be noted.

The questions and the annotations correspond to the already pre-established order of your regulated list according to the order of the priorities that you consider convenient. You will continue to ask one more time, according to the list of Iré, and if the answers are positive, you will be in the presence of a perfect Iré without any problems.

From this moment on you will only have to determine who or what is causing your luck, or who or what is benefiting you. But if in the questions' game, some or all of the results were negative, the Iré will be imperfect and the good fortune will be incomplete. In these cases, the Santero is responsible for remedying the situation until they obtain a complete Iré.

If the letter has a negative content and it does not answer to any of the Osobbos when delivering the ibó, it will have to be determined if the negativity comes from the Orishás. This may be due to some bad behavior of the client, the lack of fulfillment of a promise, a religious fault, or simply because the Saints turn their back on the consultant as karma's compensation.

If there is no correlation between the questions and the answers, it will be asked if the negativity comes from some disembodied spirit. The priest asks, "*Lariche?*" asking the Saint if he wants to say something, communicate something, or talk.

If in these cases there is a refusal on the part of the Orishá, it is asked: "*Ki Lase?*" referring to what should be done next, or what he wants us to do.

To lighten the meaning of the letter, the Santero can ask: "*Addimú?*" referring to whether an Orishá wants to receive a small offering, or "*Ebó Churé?*" when the offering is of greater caliber in quality or quantity. Or if it's simple but it's carried out immediately and in the same day, "*Ebó Keún?*" which is a progressive way in days—it can be done today or tomorrow, something, a small portion of the offerings or a small piece of what is going to be destined and offered.

If none of these questions is satisfactory, the person will have to do ebó. The ebós vary according to the Odú, the Saint who speaks in him, and the Santero's working habits. There are innumerable ebós for each case in particular.

Orungá: The First Fortune-Teller

The legends tell us that the first Babalawo, or fortune-teller, was called Orungá, who had received all the secrets of Bará Elegguá, an Orishá also known by the names of Elebba, Elegbaram, or simply Bará.

Bará, who had great sympathy for the Oracles, had gone to Ifá to ask him for all the erós (great secrets), arguing that he had to stay alert while guarding the entrances of towns and villages. He had to know the future of humankind to be able to anticipate events preventing any inconvenience.

Ifá seemed satisfied with Elegbara's pretensions and thought them justifiable. But as a condition, he asked him to bring him ten cola nuts. Elegbara searched all the roads until he realized that in the only place where there was a tree with those fruits (*obí*), was at his friend's house, Orungá.

Elegbara was determined to achieve his goals and went to the house of his friend to ask him for some obí and Orungá accepted without problems but with one condition: After Bará Elegguá learned all the mysteries and secrets, he had to show them to him.

So it was that Orungá entered into the prophetic mysteries. He loved that task and he liked to play it always accompanied by his wife Orishábi, who took care of and carried his divination tools where her husband used his fortune-telling skills.

The fame of Orungá spread throughout Africa and became known to all peoples and kingdoms. Due to its prestige, in Nigeria the Babalawos are always accompanied by their wives, who are called *Apetebí*, and in case of illness or death, the wives are replaced by the mother of the Awo.

Use of Obi in Divination

The divination that employs cola nuts or obí is usually carried out on a white plate, preferably of earthenware or mud according to the Orishá regent of the priest who is performing this procedure. Often these dishes have a colored border that varies according to the nation, the unique line of worship within Africanism, and the Holy Rector or guardian angel of the consultant. Other times, the four parts of the cola nuts are thrown on a white cloth that some priests embroider with lace as an offering to honor their Orishá. In cases when fabrics are decorated, you'll usually also find the name of the bearer or guides embroidered to one side with very fine threads and corresponding colors.

This type of divination is done in the Holy Room where the obí is cut into four parts. Because it's a sacred fruit, Agó (permission) is requested from the Orishás. The inner part is related to the open area of the obí and the outer part to the closed area. It is known and interpreted as open when the inner part falls up and closed when the outer part falls up.

Possible Combinations

Alafia: If the four pieces land open or with their inner part up, the answer of the Orishá is a resounding yes.

Oyeku or Oyako: If the four pieces land with the outside up, the answer is negative, disapproving the question. Misfortune.

Okanran or Okaran: If three pieces land closed and one open, or three external pieces land up and one down, your response is not favorable.

Eji Alaketo: If the pieces land two closed and two open, or two external pieces up and two internal pieces up, your response is positive.

Etawa: If a piece lands with one closed side and three open sides, or an outside part face up and three face down, your answer is a weak yes. You should rephrase the question.

If the pieces of Obí fall on top of each other, they represent confusion and disorder. They're perceiving the influence of Eshú and do not open the way for communication and the answers of the Orishás. You'll have to start from the beginning, asking again, honoring the messenger, Eshú, beforehand. If the answer is not positive, you could ask again but not more than three times.

Two male and two female parts are recognized in the obí, which gives us the possibility of ten more combinations in the reading. These are the resulting ten rolls:

1. **One male part open:** Idarau-Ijara

   Meaning = salvation, victory, triumph, successes

2. **One female part open:** Ajé

   Meaning = wealth, economic prosperity,
   money, good finances

3. **One male and one female part open:** Ejiré

   Meaning = friendship, fellowship, fraternity,
   sociability, union of forces

4. **Two male parts open:** Ako Oram

   Meaning = crime, fights, struggles, confrontations,
   disputes, aggression

5. **Two female parts open:** Yeié-Orán or Tabí-Aylag-Bará

   Meaning = weakness, weakening, loss of strength,
   losses in general

6. **Two male parts and two female parts open:** Akita

   Meaning = success after going through
   adversities and disturbances

7. **Two female parts and two male parts open:** Obí-Itá

   Meaning = neutrality in the message; repeat

8. **Two male parts and two female parts:** Offún-Tabí-Alafia.

   Meaning = all is well, good development of all things

9. **Landing all closed:** Qddí-Idimó

   Meaning = obstacles, inconveniences, delays, disturbances

10. **Landing all the parts on top of each other:**

    Meaning = This is seen as sloppy form and has the same
    meaning as the roll above. The value and meaning are
    recognized and can be called with the same name.

···• **P R A Y E R   T O   T H E   O B Í** •···

Agó Idara Obí
Orí Bori Olodé
Obí Unlá Babá
'Orí Bori Olodé
Obí Ero Maferefun Nilé

~~

Method with the Alubosa

Alubosa in the Yoruba language means "onion," and when used in Africanism, it performs one of the simplest known divination techniques.

To begin consulting with this method, the priest sits on the floor, where previously he will have accommodated a piece of cloth, preferably of white cotton. On one side the priest places a lighted candle and at the other end a transparent glass of water.

When the priest is ready, he or she invokes the protection and consent of Oshossi using a new (unused by everything but divination) sharp steel knife to cut the onion in half, trying to make it as perfect as possible, leaving the two parts almost equal. Who responds to this method are the *Caboclos*, and their answers are firmly and without hesitation: yes, no, or maybe. The Caboclos are very elevated spirits with spiritual light that have belonged to Native Americans. They are recognized and manifested within some groups of Afro-Brazilians with this name.

It will only respond with those three answers. If you have any doubts with respect to the interpretation, ask them again using a new onion. Although it seems almost rudimentary, it is a very fast, straightforward, and common system. Their yes answers are very concise and at the same time very precise. Questions can be asked out loud or mentally. It's important to have a high level of mental concentration at all times without ignoring the main objective.

If the two halves of the onion fall up, the answer is yes. If the two halves are down, the answer it's a no. And if they fall one down and the other up, the answer is maybe.

The Oracle with the Four Pieces of Coconut
Legend of the Oracle of Biagué

The use of coconut as an element for divination is perhaps one of the most used within Santería by its worshippers. Most of their ceremonies are certified by this system. It is also known as Oracle of Biagué, who is believed to have been a great fortune-teller, the first to use this oracle and teach it to his son, who latter on made it the most popular among the Yorubas.

The old Santeros say that one day in the beginning of Creation, Olofi came down to Earth to make sure that all things were working well and that everything was in harmony and nothing missing so the three kingdoms—the mineral, the vegetable, and the animal—could coexist in total harmony and collaborate with each other to evolve spiritually.

Walking around, he suddenly spotted a very large tree that seemed to be very far from the others. Its gorgeous shapes and very vivacious green color notably caught his attention. Seeing its size, he noticed that apart from having a very attractive shape, it was also very tall. But when he examined it more closely, he could see that such a beauty was missing something in order to be almost perfect. The branches had no fruit.

Very intrigued, he asked:

—*What are you doing there?*

The tree answered:

—*Me, sir? I move and play with the wind as the wind plays with my branches.*

—*And what would you like to do?*

—*I would like to be like the others of my kind. All have some fruit that they deliver, and I ... nothing.*

—Let me see what we can do about it. I know, each of my children has a special fruit that belongs to them, as well as a plant, a flower... but not all trees bear fruit and that is why you are more united, keeping deep secrets and Aché. I will then put that fruit in you! You are so tall that, if you want, you can reach the sky. You are so green that you represent life and hope, and you are so humble that you silently awaited the arrival of this day. Yes, I will, and to your fruit I will call: Obí Güi Güi. And it will be Obatalá, so white, as will be your fruit inside, who will communicate this to the other Orishás.

With the first rays of the sun, very early in the morning, Obatalá presided over a consul and told the others:

—Here in front of you is the fruit that will speak for all of us. Its name is Obí Güi Güi, fruit of the palm and direct creation of Olofi. She, by mandate of Him, will answer all the questions and reveal all the secrets of the pure hands that separate it in four parts and throw their pieces in search of our voice.

Soon after, everyone began to learn to read the coconuts thanks to Obatalá. The story goes that it was a long time before a man with pure hands and the innocence of a child arrived, who retained his authority and maturity and knew how to engender in his being the innate strength of the fortune-tellers. His name was Biagué and he had a single son named Adiatotó who inherited from his father the respect and knowledge of the Oracle.

After the death of Biagué, his adopted children appropriated all the things that legally belong to Adiatotó, leaving nothing to him but the true inheritance of his father: his incorruptible honesty and the coconut symbols of this virtue.

Time passed but the discomfort caused by the betrayal of those he had considered his stepbrothers did not end. Mired in sadness, he could do nothing.

After losing all his belongings, the king of the village ordered to investigate the lands that Adiatotó said had belonged to his father. Finding no documents to prove it, he ordered the fortune-teller's son to be called and said:

> —*If it is true that you are Adiatotó, and that you are the legitimate son of the Awo Biagué, then you can answer all my questions through the coconuts. And as certain as your answers are, it will be true that you are the true owner of those lands.*

Thus, the son of the fortune-teller answered one by one all the king's questions for several days, without resting. When the monarch confirmed that Adiatotó did not lie, because the coconuts never lie, after answering with exact precision and truthfulness to all his questions, the lands passed to his true owner who, from that moment on, never forgot to practice divination with the coconuts every day.

Method of Divination with the Coconut

To carry out the divination, get a healthy and dry coconut and then apply the necessary blows in the center of the fruit until it breaks into four pieces. Then, separate the pieces and clean them with fresh water.

Use a heavy tool to break it, like a hammer, holding the fruit with one of your hands with great respect and care. Never throw or crash the coconut on the floor (unless the ritual requires it) because many of the older and more orthodox practitioners consider it a very serious fault.

If you do not have much experience, start the ritual by asking questions only of Elegguá. Little by little you will gain experience and will be able to ask questions to the other Orishás. Before starting the interpretation, it is necessary to follow some steps that have to do with the ritual and that are carried out by all the priests. If you're not a priest, speak to the Saint in your usual way, in your language and with your idioms that he will understand. Do not forget that you are venturing into a sacred divination system and therefore must do it with utmost seriousness and respect.

The Santero begins with invocations in the Yoruba language saying:

> —*Bogguo Iworo Iyalorishá Babalorihá Babalawo Oluo Olorí Awon ti a te ni Ifá Awo Ikú Embelesse Ibaé Baié Tonu Bogguo Iworo Awoses.*

This prayer is a tribute and is dedicated to the Santeros and Babalawos who have passed away in order that they may rest in peace. Then they name all those who were very important when they occupied those positions (Santeros and Babalawos) in the field of divination.

They say the following:

—*Awoses Fun Mi Ni Ifá*

This means "Bring me Wisdom." They go on to say:

—*Kosi Ikú Kosi Ikú Loghí Kosi Ofó Kosi Ano Atotó Aikú Babagwa.*

That means: "There may be no death, there may be no death or grave, there may be no losses of loved ones, there may be no disease. Keep them away and let good and eternal things come."

Then greetings are given to the godparents. saying:

—*Kinkamashé Iya re mi, Kinkamashé Oyurbona mi Agó.*

In this way, the person and the position he represents are greeted by symbolically requesting permission to continue. Later, water is sprayed three times in front of the Orishá that is going to be consulted (in the case of the example to Elegguá) and they recite:

—*Omí Tutu Ana Tutu Omí Tutu Awo Ilé Elegguá.*

The Santero continues to tear off pieces of the white pulp with his hands from each of the four pieces of coconut destined for divination, the time of which is depending on their quantity, the number that corresponds to the Orishá invoked, and the order of the different Odús.

The small pieces of coconut are put in the place of enlightenment and settlement of the Saint, sometimes making syncretism meaningful, on the crossed images that have followed the same treatment that is given to necklaces or guides, for example.

In these moments you can say:

—*Si Elegguá Éyi Obí Jówo Wá Fun Mi Ni Iré.*

This means: "this coconut is for Elegguá. Please come and give me good fortune." The floor is then struck three times with the closed fists of the right hand (form of greeting and call for Elegguá). Finally, the pieces of coconut are taken between the two hands and brought up to the chest height, saying:

—*Obí Si Elegguá.*

Then the four pieces of the fruit are thrown. Before they fall, you say:

—*Ashé.*

This is to implicitly attract the idea of strength and power, wishing that it were so.

Interpretation of the Five Rolls of the Coconut
Alafia

When its four parts fall facing up (white part up), its answer is yes. To confirm the outcome, it is necessary to ask again. If Alafia answers yes again, it is confirmed. If the second time the answer is Okana Sode or Oyeku, your answer is totally negative or bad. But if it answers with Ejife or Etawa, it is positive or good.

Oyeku or Oyekun

When the four pieces of coconut fall with their dark side facing upwards, the answer is no. It also carries a highly disastrous meaning. This position speaks of death. There the priest must ask whether the Oracle is talking *to* him, or *through* him, to the consultants.

Here the Orishás speak firmly and no further clarification is needed. The priest must replace the pieces of coconut, as if wanting to purify them from the influence of the answer, before asking again. He or she who is recording with the coconut should touch the ground with the index finger and middle of the right hand, bring them together to their lips and kiss them. Then touching his forehead between the eyebrows and finally, on the upper back part of the head, asking for *Maleme* (Mercy) to the Orishás and his Saint with his head. Then they will say:

—*Obí Iré*—*eó* (I ask that whatever comes is good).

Then he or she continues saying, while touching the ground beforehand again:

—*Moffin Karé, Moffin Karé Godó, Dafa Moffin Karé Godó Baé.*

—*Alafia Kisí Ekó, Alafia Beké Lorié Ennacan Orí mi Aferé Assaka Beké Owuaní.*

—*Moyugba Abé Ebbámi Omá Tun Omá Esabami Miche Fun Ni Orno Ni Mi.*

In an act of profound detachment, they will elevate the thought so that the good is gathered in a healthy and clear response so that their head (energy center concentrating the spiritual and connected with the Cosmos) is free of possible disturbances and receives the protection of the Divinity.

In this instance and before continuing with the interpretation, it is necessary to know if it is an egún that is responding and wants to warn of the death of someone. Even if it were not the case, it is necessary to take a bath of abó, a sacred liquid made of macerated herbs and other secret components, to light a candle for the egúns and to do ebó immediately.

Ejife

The fall of the pieces of coconut in this roll consists of two pieces with their dark part upwards and the other two with their white part in the upward position (or two and two). This answer is one of the safest and categorical and it brings a resounding yes without needing to reiterate the question.

Etawa

This roll occurs when three of the pieces of coconut land with their white side up and the fourth with the dark side up. Your answer is a yes, but to be granted you must secure it with some kind of ebó. The consultant will have to repeat the question by verifying that everything has gone well to corroborate the answers.

Okana Sode

This roll is three pieces of coconut with its black parts upwards and one white piece upwards. Your answer is a no. It's advisable to review the procedure because there is the possibility of having made a mistake. It speaks of some negative or pernicious influence for the one who consults.

Afterword

Mandate of Oran-Niyán

Black and white men of, together and linked.
Knowledge and action, wisdom and technique.
Inspiration and intuition.
The sunrise and the sunset in search of the sun and the moon.
With the only one and same God.
With the same origin and the same purpose.

In a cosmic and magical moment at the beginning of the creative spark on Earth, Oddudduá (light skin) and Ogún (dark skin) shared love for the same woman.

Father and son were hopelessly in love with the same feminine essence.

Ogún's weapons and iron possessed her illegitimately, seized and kidnapped her thoughts, and captured her sentimentally, while the power of Oddudduá subjugated her until he almost hypnotized her completely.

One contains the other (the earth contains iron), but both the father and the son desire the same in a carnal way.

From this love triangle, Oran-niyán was born, half-black and half-white, and he became one of the seven principal princes who existed at the beginning of the world.

Oran-niyán is known in mythology as the founder of the Oyó dynasty, who then excelled politically and militarily over the other kingdoms.

By inheritance of his two parents, he owned the iron, the land, and the mandate of Olofi to separate the waters and create the safe ground that emerged from the waters.

Then the waters separated from the air (considered as the beginning of life, which represented the breath of creation, symbolizing the sky at its best) until the terrestrial layers were created as the beginning of the life of the beings incarnated in the world.

They were the first seven princes who, with divine attributes and special characteristics, possessed immense riches, and each of them fostered an active principle of life.

According to the bible, speaking figuratively, they could be related to the seven days of creation where the Creator rested on the seventh day.

The seventh prince was Oran-niyán, who by supra-terrestrial mandates would be configured as indispensable and would represent a seventh stage where stability and balance were already in operation and the peace of the deserved rest had been established.

The world came from two entities (their parents) but it took a third part that, symbolically represented by a chicken, would hatch an egg as a symbol of life.

This bird would trample the earth, and with its beak would scatter it over the waters, and Oran-niyán, like Obatalá with his magical sack received from Olofi, would remove the earth from the bag and scatter it among the seas.

The cult has been lost, but many believe that because the origin of the theory is more divine than privileged, it is perhaps a passage from our Obatalá (Oxalá or Oxalaguían) who wields a silver sword with iron alloys descending from Oxalufán (the most ancestral).

This legend has lost its current power because Obatalá is credited with the function of spreading enough land from its magical bag to create the first islands and continents. However, I wanted to rescue this ancient African legend to highlight the union that should never be lost between black and white people or between any other ethnic groups, and as proof and desire of the Orishás, so that both peoples (and those of other races) unite for the evolution of the human being.

Appendix: Resources for the Odús

Different Names for the Odús

Here is a list of names of the Odús given by different Saint Houses. It can be important to know all the versions of the names of the Odús. It is ordered by numerical ordination according to the number of open seashells.

1	Okaran	Okana	Ocana
2	Ejioko	Eyioko	Ejioko
3	Etaogunda	Oggundá	Ogundá
4	Orosun	Iroso	Yroso
5	Oxe	Oché	Osé
6	Obara	Oddí Obba	Obara
7	Odí	Oddí	Odí
8	Ejionile	Eyéunle	Ejéunle
9	Osa	Osá	Osá
10	Ofu	Ofún—Mafún	Offún
11	Owarin	Ojuani—Chobe	Ojuani
12	Ejilas Sebora	Eyila—Chebora	Eyinlá
13	Eji—Ologbon	Metanlá	Metanlá
14	Iká	Merinlá	Merinlá
15	Ori—Baba—Baja	Marunlá	Marunlá
16	Alafia	Merindiloggún	Mediloggún

List of Names in Diloggún and Ifá

Here is a list of the names of the Odús in Diloggún and Ifá, correspondingly. They are listed numerically by the number of open seashells.

#	Diloggún	Ifá
1	Okana	Okana Meji
2	Ejioko	Oyekún Meji
3	Ogundá	Ogundá Meji
4	Iroso	Iroso Meji
5	Oché	Oché Meji
6	Obara	Obara Meji
7	Odí	Odí Meji
8	Ejéunle	Eyiogbe Meji
9	Osá	Osá Meji
10	Ofún	Ofún Meji
11	Ojuani	Ojuaní Meji
12	Eyila Chebora	Otrupo Meji
13	Metanlá	Irete Meji
14	Merinlá	Iká Meji
15	Marunlá	Iwori Meji
16	Merindiloggún	Otura Meji

Meji of the Odús

The sixteen Odús are composed of sixteen letters that are called the Meji, under the conceptualization of the double, the number two. They are known as Odús of Ifá and their representation is as follows:

Okana Meji
```
II II
II II
II II
 I  I
```

Oyekún Meji
```
II II
II II
II II
II II
```

Ogundá Meji
```
 I  I
 I  I
 I  I
II II
```

Iroso Meji
```
 I  I
 I  I
II II
II II
```

Oché Meji
```
 I  I
II II
 I  I
II II
```

Obara Meji
```
 I  I
II II
II II
II II
```

Odí Meji
```
 I  I
II II
II II
 I  I
```

Eyiogbe Meji
```
 I  I
 I  I
 I  I
 I  I
```

Osá Meji
```
II II
 I  I
 I  I
 I  I
```

Ofún Meji
```
II II
 I  I
II II
 I  I
```

Ojuani Meji
```
II II
II II
 I  I
 I  I
```

Otrupo Meji
```
II II
II II
 I  I
II II
```

Irete Meji
```
 I  I
 I  I
II II
 I  I
```

Iká Meji
```
II II
 I  I
II II
II II
```

Iwori Meji
```
II II
 I  I
 I  I
II II
```

Otura Meji
```
 I  I
II II
 I  I
 I  I
```

The Sayings of the Odús

1. Okana

"The beginning started through the Unity, the driving force of the one, and that's how the World began. From there on, if the good does not exist, there is no evil."

2. Ejioko

"Rivalry between brothers: an arrow between them."

3. Ogundá

"Fights, disputes and discussion: they confuse and bring tragedies."

4. Iroso

"It's unknown what exists in the depths of the sea."

5. Oché

"Blood is life; they both run through arteries and veins. Blood and life are one thing. For this function to take place, your heart pumps, and the uninterrupted flow of life does not end."

6. Obara

"A true monarch does not rule with lies."

7. Odí

"At the beginning there was a huge hole. Then, where the hole was, it filled with water."

8. Ejéunle

"The head directs the body. There is only one monarch for the people, and only one head in a body."

9. Osá

"Your best friend is also your worst enemy."

10. Ofún

"Where the curse comes from."

11. Ojuani

"Transporting water with a straw basket is not very profitable."

12. Eyila Chebora

"Wake up, otherwise you will lose the war. Courage will be your ally!"
"Be orderly and not restless or unruly, otherwise and in spite of everything, they will manage to defeat you."

13. Metanlá

"The illness comes from the sickness of the blood."

14. Merinlá

"Be fair and measured, without doing more or less, but fair and impartial."

15. Marunlá

"You can use the path to walk or to stop. On the path you could follow or be followed. You can walk or stop, however, it will always be a path."

16. Merindiloggún

"A wise man is the one who knows how to listen, and a good ruler knows how to respect the requests and needs of his people. The wise governs the heads of all and does not ignore the ancestral voice of the oracle."

Glossary

Abó: Liquid of sacred character made of macerated herbs and secret components destined for spiritual healing, purification baths, and crossing guides against kiumbas (darkened spirits). The liquid is used to wash all the things that may be inside a Holy room (before entering the place) to remove any negative vibration that could come from the outside world.

Abóbora or Jerimum: Fruit of the *aboboreira* (family of *cucurbitaceae*).

Adjá: Musical instrument similar to metal bells in the form of elongated cones that end together in a single handle. They are used in most rituals. Its color and metal may vary according to the Orishá who is being interpreted. For example, they can be gold or bronze colored sheets for Oshún and copper for Iansá or Oyá.

Agá: Permission or license in the form of a greeting offered to the Orishás.

Agôgô: Two elongated metal cones, one longer than the other, similar to two bells that are joined by a handle in U-shape. It is struck with a metal rod to produce a high vibratory frequency sound very appropriate for religious-spiritual purposes.

Alabé: Function usually exercised by an ogá who is in charge of directing the percussionists in the "touches for the Saints" (religious celebrations.)

Alubosa: Onion.

Apetebí: Priestess who accompanies and acts with the Babalawo.

Ariashé: Herbal baths made for the initiates as a very important part of their spiritual purification.

Ashé: Also known as Aché or Axé. It implies strength, grace, or power.

Babá: Father.

Babalawo: "Father of the secret." Priest prepared and expert in the art of divination. Religious sages dedicated to the Tabla de Ifá. Priests consecrated to Ifá.

Babalorishá or Babalocha: Father of the Saints.

Babanla: Grandfather, Supreme father, or Great father.

Barracao: Place where public ceremonies are held in Afro-Brazilian Santería.

Búzios: Name of the cowrie seashells in Brazil and in countries where it has religious influence.

Corojo oil or butter: Concentrated oil used in the Afro-Cuban Santería. It is similar to dendé oil. Oil substance widely used in offerings, meals of the Orishás and ebós.

Cowrie Seashells: Gastropod mollusk usually brought from the African west coast.

Cyprea Moneta: Scientific name of cowrie seashells.

Dadá: Orishá little revered. Feminine principle of energy that took care of midwives of mothers and babies at the time of breastfeeding, protecting them from diseases and fortifying their health. One of the known religious syncretism is with Our Lady of the Rosary.

Deká: Religious ceremony and act by which the office of Babalorishá or Iyalorishá is received in the presence of other high priests who confirm and publicly verify its validity.

Dendé oil: See corojo oil or butter.

Diloggún: Abbreviation of the term: "Merindiloggún."

Dobalé: Reverential greeting made by the Sons of Saint who have an assigned female Orishá.

Ebó: Magical work and offerings for the Orishás within Santería.

Ebomin: Woman with more than seven years of practice in the "Law of the Saint."

Efún: Type of white clay used as a paint to design religious characters.

Egún: Spirit of the dead.

Egungún: In "Nagó," means bone or soul of a dead person. Skeleton.

Ekedé: Position held by the woman as an assistant to the mediums in moments of trance with an Orishá. Woman who dresses and attend the Orishás.

Epó: Dendé oil, and any oily substance in general.

Eró: Secret.

Fá: Ifá, for the Jejes.

Father of Saint: Babalorishá or Babalocha. Known in Brazil commonly with the name of "Pai de Santo."

Fun Fun: Cold, white.

Guardian Angel: Spiritual guide. Common name of someone's Orishá's guide. That person is your spiritual son. Also known as Orishá head or front.

Holy room: Place where the settlements of the Orishás are found along with their tools and belongings. Room considered sacred by the energies that dwell there. Superior forces of the good and the light.

Iaó: Also known as Iyawó or Yawó. It means initiated in the religion.

Ifé: Ancestral center. City of Nigeria that stood out as reign. Also known as the territory of Ifé: Ilé Ifé. It means love. Religious center of the Yorubas.

Iká: A reverential greeting made by the Sons of Saint ruled by a male Orishá.

Ikís: Oracle belonging to Orulá.

Ikú: Death.

Ilé: Residence, territory, land, house. Place where you reside or live or someone's home.

Italero: Santero specialized in reading with cowrie seashells.

Iyá: Mother.

Iylabá: General designation given to any female Orishá.

Iyalorishá: Mother of the Saints also known as Iyalocha in Afro-Cuban and Caribbean Santería.

Iyanlá: Grandmother, supreme mother or great mother.

Iyá-Ifá: Classification given in Nigeria to women who work in divination (as mothers of a process of transformation into prophetic levels).

Karma: "Law of cause and effect." Universal law compensatory of good or bad actions, based on another law also of universal character called "Law of reincarnation."

Kiss or revere the stone: Similar action to one above, but in front of the consecrated Otás.

Kiumbas: Spirits of disturbing dead left behind that suffered in life of serious defects. They could have been murderers, rapists, swindlers, etc., and they have had a high negative content. When disembodied they form a very low spiritual category dedicated to disturb incarnate beings. They are obsessive, persecute and foment low passions, and often they are the driving force of black or negative magic.

Kola: Cola nut. Fruit used in religion.

Lucumí: Also known as "Ulcumis" or people from the regions near the Niger Delta. The word "Lukkami" melted into Lucumí. They lived in the kingdom of Oyó or Ulkama, which is another of the largest political and religious centers. In Cuba it means all the tribes that identified with the Yoruba language during the slave trade in that country.

Make Saint: Act where someone enters into the "Law of the Saint." Receive and settle your Orishá of head. Your Guardian Angel. Begin in Santería.

Mother of Saint: Iyalorishá or Iyalocha. Religious expression with borders of affection and maternal love due to his tutelary status toward his children of Saint. In Brazil it is popularly known as "Maes de Santo."

Manu: Number 5.

Manulá: Number 15.

Medium: A person with the faculty of being the bridge between the material and the spiritual world and uses "mediumship" for that purpose.

Mediumship: Also called or known as the "Sixth Sense." Psychic faculty that allows the individual to communicate with the "Beyond."

Méfa: Number 6.

Mégua: Number 10.

Melle: Number 7.

Mellela: Number 17.

Melli: Number 2.

Mellilá: Number 12.

Melli meguá: Number 20.

Méllo: Number 8.

Mellolá: Number 18.

Mérin: Number 4.

Merinlá: Number 14.

Meta: Number 3.

Metalá: Number 13.

Mésan: Number 9.

Mesanlá: Number 19.

Nations: Different lines of worship within the Yoruban Africanism. It can vary in certain particularities but never in its bases or essence maintaining always the same basic foundations in the cult.

Obá: King.

Obí: African fruit, the cola nut.

Obí Güi Güi: Coconut.

Odús: Letters. Each one of the different readings and/or throws determined in Ifá or in the Diloggún.

Ogá: Person chosen by the priest in a medium-psychic trance state (with his Orishá incorporated or with his Orishá in the earth), or by some other person of certain prestige and importance within the cult and who acts in identical circumstances. Position of honor created for many purposes, for example, to establish civilly a good relationship between the temple and society.

Igbo: The items or elements that intervene at the beginning of the process of divination. The consultant holds them in one hand. They are part of the Igbo, a small stone called otá, a guacalote seed that receives the name of Egué Alió or Ewe Ayó; a small and long white snail called Alié or Aye; a doll head that is called Erí-Aguona or Erí-Aworan; and the small and generally rounded-shaped portion of husk, called efún.

Okanchocho: Number 1.

Ologberi: Territory or portion of the unknown inhabited by people from other towns. Lands or unknown places. The foreigners.

Omiero: Liquid considered sacred made with rainwater, seawater, river water, honey, herbs, and other elements.

Orno: Son.

Orí: Head. Also, oily substance of rather dense consistency, such as fat or butter or ointment, of a rather clear color extracted from the cotton pits. It is used in specific rituals such as the magnetization of the tools of each Orishá.

Orí inú: Part considered as the most sacred area of the head regulating psychic activity.

Orishás funfun: "The cold." People with the most calm, serene and peaceful personality. It's the opposite of Orishás Gbigbona.

Orishás Gbigbona: "The hot." People of great temperament and character. Impetuous and mostly male.

Orita Goal: Line or point of intersection that separates and at the same time unites the Orún and the Aye.

Orogbó: African fruit used in rituals.

Orún: "The other world." World of invisible, intangible or abstract things.

Otá: Stone that according to its characteristics is destined to one or another Orishá to make its "settlement" on it and becoming a receptacle for the forces of nature. They are magnetic seats and act as connecting elements attracting the beneficial action of the Orishás.

Patakkí: Tales of legends and myths related to the stories of the Orishás with moralizing lessons tending to spiritual perfection. Their interpretations explain each of the letters or Odús.

Paxoró: Staff or scepter of Oxalá or Obatalá. It represents his power on earth.

Santería: Devotion to the Saints. Religion of the Orishás in America.

Son of Saint: Person initiated in the cult of the Orishás.

Stir head: Expression commonly used to describe the action of lying on the floor and gently support the head generally with the intention of requesting license ("Agó") to religious superiors and prostrating at the feet of the elderly with great respect.

Taramesso: Table on which the Priest consults with the seashells.

Terreiro: House of Religion or Temple of the Afro-Brazilian Santería.

Vodum: Similar to Orishá for the Candomblés who keep purely the religious concepts of the Jejes (people who emigrated from Dahomé and today is the People's Republic of Benin).

Vumbe: Denomination given to the set of souls or to that of the spirits of the ancestors.

Xaxará or Shashará: Omulú's symbol made of a material similar to raffia similar to his mother Naná Burukú.

Zambi: Another Olorun designation. God for the religious descendants of the Angola region.

Bibliography

Adivinos y Oráculos Griegos. Robert Flaceliere. EUDEBA, 1993.

Awo: Ifá and the Theology of Orishá Divination. Awo Fá ' Lokun Fatunmbi. Original Publication.

Beaded Splendor. National Museum of African Art. Smithsonian Institution. Washington, DC, 1994.

Civilizaciones de Occidente. Su Historia y su Cultura. Tomo 1. Edward Me. Nall Burns. Ediciones Siglo Veinte, 1980.

Componentes Africanos en el Etnos Cubano. Rafael L. López Valdés. Etnología. Editorial de Ciencias Sociales: La Habana, 1985.

Dieux d 'Afrique. Guite des Orishás et Vodouns a 1' ancienne Cóte des Esclaves en Afrique et a Bahia, la Baie de Tous les Saints au Brésil. Pierre Fátúmbí Verger. Éditions Revue Naire: París, 1995.

Diloggún. Oráculo de Obatalá. Cecilio Pérez. Oba Ecun Books, 1986.

El Arte de tirar los Caracoles e interpretar los Cocos. Los oráculos de Biague y Dialoggun (Folklores Afro—Cubano.) Language Research Press.

El Oráculo de los Cauris. Hablan los Caracoles. J. A. Sáenz Astort. Alfadil Ediciones, 1994.

*El Santo (La Ocha.) Secretos de la Religió*n Lucumí. Julio García Cortez. Editora Latino Americana, S. A, 1976.

El Secreto de la Santería. La Enciclopedia Yoruba Lucumí. Carlos Guzman. 1984. The Latín Press Publishing Co: New York.

El Tarot de los Orishás. Zolrak & Durkon. Woodbury: Llewellyn Publications, 1994.

Gods of the Yoruba. Lowie Museum of Anthropology. University of California, Berkeley, 1979.

Historia Universal. Grecia. Carl Grimberg y Ragnar Svanstrom. Círculo de Lectores S. A, 1986.

Ifá. Antigua Sabiduría. Oba Ecun. Oba Ecun Books, 1993.

Jogo de Búzios. Lenda e realidade. Ronaldo Antonio Linares. Tríade Editorial.

La Esclavitud en Hispanoamérica. Rolando Mellafé. EUDEBA. 1987.

Los Caracoles. Historia de sus Letras. Andres R. Rogers. Editado por Librería Latinoamericana, 1973.

Los Orishás en Cuba. Natalia Bolívar Aróstegui. Ediciones Unión, Unión de Escritores y Artistas de Cuba, 1990.

Manual de Orihate. Religión Lucumí. Nicolás Valentín Angarica.

Mitología. Guía ilustrada de los Mitos del Mundo. Doctor Roy Willis (Introducción; Grandes temas de la mitología Africana y varios. Editor Roy Willis. DEBATE. Círculo de Lectores.

O Destino Revelado no Jogo de Búzios. Jorge Alberto Varanda. Editora ECO.

O Jogo de Búzios. A sorte e o destino revelados pelo Jogo de Búzios. Fernandes Portugal. Ediouro. Grupo Coquetel.

O Jogo dos Búzios e as Grandes Cerimónias ocultas da Umbanda. 4a Edición. José Ribeiro de Souza. Editora Espiritualista Ltda.

O Jogo dos Búzios. Dr. Byron Torres de Freitas. Editora ECO. 8a Edición.

O Verdadeiro Jogo dos Búzios. Babalawó Oju-Obá Editora ECO, 1972.

Santería. Magia Africana en Latinoamérica. Migene González Wippler. Editorial Diana, 1976.

Summa Artis. Historia General del Arte. Tomo V. José Pijoan. Espasa Calpe S.A. 1953.

Suma Teologica (1A. Ed.). Tomas de Aquino, S. Madrid: Biblioteca de Autores Cristianos, 1964.

Tem Dende tem Axé. Etnografia do Dendezeiro. Raul Lody. Ed. Pallas, 1992.

Tranca Ruas Das Almas. No Candomblé e na Umbanda. José Ribeiro de Souza e Decelso. Editora ECO, 1974.

Versión Reina-Valera. Sociedades Bíblicas en América Latina, 1960. Renovado, Sociedades Bíblicas Unidas, 1988.

Yemayá y Ochún. Kariocha, Iyalorichas y Olorichas. Lydia Cabrera. Colección del Chicherukú en el exilio. Madrid, 1974.

Yoruba: Nine Centuries of African Art and Thought. Drewal, Henry John, and John Pemberton 111, with Rowland Abiodun. Edited by Allen Wardwell. New York: The Center of African Art in Association with Harry N. Abrams Inc. Publishers, 1991.

To Write to the Author

If you wish to contact the author or would like more information about this book, please write to the author in care of Llewellyn Worldwide Ltd. and we will forward your request. Both the author and the publisher appreciate hearing from you and learning of your enjoyment of this book and how it has helped you. Llewellyn Worldwide Ltd. cannot guarantee that every letter written to the author can be answered, but all will be forwarded. Please write to:

Zolrak
℅ Llewellyn Worldwide
2143 Wooddale Drive
Woodbury, MN 55125-2989

Please enclose a self-addressed stamped envelope for reply,
or $1.00 to cover costs. If outside the U.S.A., enclose
an international postal reply coupon.

Many of Llewellyn's authors have websites with additional information and resources. For more information, please visit our website at http://www.llewellyn.com.

GET MORE AT LLEWELLYN.COM

Visit us online to browse hundreds of our books and decks, plus sign up to receive our e-newsletters and exclusive online offers.

- Free tarot readings • Spell-a-Day • Moon phases
- Recipes, spells, and tips • Blogs • Encyclopedia
- Author interviews, articles, and upcoming events

GET SOCIAL WITH LLEWELLYN

Find us on 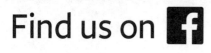  @LlewellynBooks

www.Facebook.com/LlewellynBooks

GET BOOKS AT LLEWELLYN

LLEWELLYN ORDERING INFORMATION

Order online: Visit our website at www.llewellyn.com to select your books and place an order on our secure server.

Order by phone:
- Call toll free within the US at 1-877-NEW-WRLD (1-877-639-9753)
- We accept VISA, MasterCard, American Express, and Discover.
- Canadian customers must use credit cards.

Order by mail:
Send the full price of your order (MN residents add 6.875% sales tax) in US funds plus postage and handling to: Llewellyn Worldwide, 2143 Wooddale Drive, Woodbury, MN 55125-2989

POSTAGE AND HANDLING

STANDARD (US):
(Please allow 12 business days)
$30.00 and under, add $6.00.
$30.01 and over, FREE SHIPPING.

INTERNATIONAL ORDERS,
INCLUDING CANADA:
$16.00 for one book, plus $3.00 for each additional book.

Visit us online for more shipping options. Prices subject to change.

FREE CATALOG!

To order, call
1-877-NEW-WRLD
ext. 8236
or visit our
website